Steck-Vaughn

GED

SOCIAL STUDIES

Exercise Book

STECK-VAUGHN
ELEMENTARY · SECONDARY · ADULT · LIBRARY

A Harcourt Company

ACKNOWLEDGMENTS

Executive Editor: Ellen Northcutt
Senior Editor: Donna Townsend
Associate Design Director: Joyce Spicer
Supervising Designer: Pamela Heaney
Media Researcher: Sarah Fraser

Photo Credits: Cover: (Constitution) ©Jack Zehrt/FPG International, (Monument Valley) ©The Stock Market; p. 23 ©Stuart Franklin/Magnum Photos; p. 58 ©North Wind; p. 62 ©CORBIS; p. 76 ©TimePix; p. 79 ©Bill Pierce/TimePix.

Cartoon Credits: P.11 Rob Rodgers ©United Feature Syndicate, Inc.; p.23 Jeff Danziger ©Tribune Media Services, Inc.; p.25 Jim Borgman ©King Features Syndicate; p.27 Mike Luckovich ©Creaters Syndicate, Inc; p.34 Steve McBride ©Independence Daily Reporter (Kan.); p.36 Bill Yates ©King Features Syndicate; p.41a David Cox ©NW Arkansas Morning News/Donrey Media Group; p.41b Chester Commodore ©Chicago Defender; p.44 C. Barsotti ©1989 USA Today; p.58 Ralph Dunagin ©1989 The Orlando Sentinel North American Syndicate, Inc.; p.67 David Seavey ©1989 USA Today; p.70 Hank McClure ©Lawton Constitution; p.73a Michael Ramirez ©Copley News Service; p.73b Sargent ©1989 Ausin American Statesman/Universal Press Syndicate; p.81 ©Steve Nease; p.85 Arthur A. Henrikson ©The Daily Herald.

ISBN 0-7398-3605-6

Printed in the United States of America.

6 7 8 9 10 RP 07 06 05 04 03 02

Contents

To the Learner 2

Unit 1: United States History 4

Unit 2: World History 16

Unit 3: Civics and Government 24

Unit 4: Economics 35

Unit 5: Geography 45

Simulated GED Test A 56

    Analysis of Performance: Test A...........................71

Simulated GED Test B......................................72

    Analysis of Performance: Test B............................88

Answers and Explanations 89

Answer Sheet 110

The *Steck-Vaughn GED Social Studies Exercise Book* provides you with practice in answering the types of questions found on the actual GED Social Studies Test. It can be used with the *Steck-Vaughn GED Social Studies* book or with the *Steck-Vaughn Complete GED Preparation* book. This exercise book contains both practice exercises and simulated GED tests.

Practice Exercises

The GED Social Studies Test examines your ability to understand, apply, analyze, and evaluate information in five social studies areas: United States history, world history, civics and government, economics, and geography. On the GED Test, 25 percent of the questions are about United States history, 15 percent are about world history, 25 percent are about civics and government, 20 percent are about economics, and 15 percent are about geography.

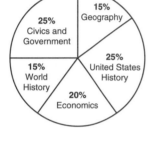

The practice exercises are divided into the same five content areas by unit. Unit 1 covers the major periods and developments in United States history from its beginnings to the present. Unit 2, world history, focuses on the major periods and developments from the beginnings of human society through the twentieth century. Unit 3 covers civics and government, including the American political system and the relationship of the United States to other nations and to world affairs. Unit 4, economics, includes economic systems, production and consumption, financial institutions, and global markets. Unit 5, geography, focuses on the regions of the world, physical and human systems, the environment, and the uses of geography to interpret the past, present, and future.

Simulated Tests

This workbook contains two full-length Simulated GED Social Studies Tests. Each Simulated Test has the same number and types of questions as the actual GED Test. All of the questions on the GED Social Studies Test are multiple choice. Each question is based on a graphic, a prose passage, or a combination of the two. Forty percent of questions rely on a prose passage only, 40 percent rely on a graphic only, and 20 percent rely on a combination of a passage and a graphic. Reading passages include excerpts from fundamental documents of the United States, such as the Declaration of Independence, and from practical documents, such as tax forms.

Questions on the test may be either single questions or part of a question set. Forty percent of the questions are single questions, and 60 percent are in question sets. In addition, 60 percent of questions relate to concepts and issues that have a global or international perspective, and 40 percent relate to concepts and issues specific to a United States setting.

The Simulated Tests can help you decide if you are ready to take the GED Social Studies Test. Take each test under the same time restrictions as you will have for the actual GED Test. For each test, complete the 50 items within 70 minutes. Space the two examinations apart by at least a week.

After each Simulated Test, a Performance Analysis Chart will help you determine if you are ready to take the GED Social Studies Test. The charts give a breakdown by content area and by question type. By completing these charts, you can determine your own strengths and weaknesses as they relate to social studies.

Cognitive Levels

Following is an explanation of the four cognitive levels of questions that you will practice in this book and that are found on the GED Test.

1. Comprehension questions require you to identify restated information or information that is paraphrased. They require you to summarize ideas, identify implications, or make inferences.

2. Application questions require you to recognize a generalization, principle, or strategy and to apply it in a new situation.

3. Analysis questions measure your ability to distinguish fact from opinion or hypotheses, differentiate conclusions and supporting statements, recognize unstated assumptions and logical fallacies, identify cause-and-effect relationships, recognize points of view, and determine the implications of presenting visual data in different ways.

4. Evaluation questions require the ability to make judgments about how adequate, appropriate, valid, or accurate a set of data, methods, or conclusions may be. They include comparing and contrasting different accounts of the same event and recognizing the role of values and beliefs in decision making.

The questions on the GED Test are 20 percent comprehension, 20 percent application, 40 percent analysis, and 20 percent evaluation.

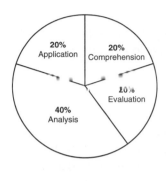

Graphics

Visual processing skills are very important on the GED Social Studies Test. As many as 60 percent of the test questions may be based on graphics either used alone or in combination with a prose passage. Included are maps, graphs, diagrams, charts, tables, political cartoons, and photographs. Practice in recognizing biases and assumptions in graphics and in understanding the relationship of data within a visual or between a visual and prose data is essential to develop the skills you need on the test.

Answers

The answer section gives explanations of why an answer is correct and why the other answer choices are incorrect. Sometimes by studying the reason an answer is incorrect, you can learn to avoid a similar problem in the future.

Correlation Chart

The following correlation chart shows how the sections of this exercise book relate to sections of other Steck-Vaughn GED preparation books. You can refer to these two books for further instruction or review.

CONTENT AREAS	United States History	World History	Civics and Government	Economics	Geography
BOOK TITLES *Steck-Vaughn GED Exercise Book*	Unit 1	Unit 2	Unit 3	Unit 4	Unit 5
Steck-Vaughn GED Social Studies Exercise Book	Unit 1	Unit 2	Unit 3	Unit 4	Unit 5
Steck-Vaughn Complete GED Preparation	Unit 3, United States History	Unit 3, World History	Unit 3, Civics and Government	Unit 3, Economics	Unit 3, Geography

Directions: Choose the one best answer to each question.

Questions 1 through 4 refer to the following passage and map.

Christopher Columbus, an Italian, sailed the ocean in 1492 in search of a westward route from Spain to India. He not only was the first European to travel to the Americas, but he also started further exploration that eventually led to the colonization of the Americas. Spain, England, France, Holland, and Portugal all colonized the Americas. Columbus claimed the West Indies for Spain, and Italian John Cabot (Giovanni Caboto) claimed Newfoundland in 1497 for England. Yet a third Italian, Amerigo Vespucci, was sent by Spain in 1499 to sail along part of the South American coast. He was followed during the next forty years by other explorers claiming land for the Spanish Crown.

Colonization as of 1784

PACIFIC OCEAN

Caribbean Sea

Equator

ATLANTIC OCEAN

Portuguese territory

Spanish territory

British territory

Scale at the Equator
0   2000 Miles
0   2000 Kilometers

1. Which of the following statements is best supported by the passage?

   (1) All the explorers found what they were looking for.
   (2) European sailors were in search of adventure.
   (3) Italians were skilled navigators.
   (4) Trade routes to India were finally discovered.
   (5) The world is round.

2. Which of the following statements about Europe is supported by the passage?

   (1) Although France and England had been rivals, they now embarked on a policy of cooperation.
   (2) Because Italy was not a strong, unified country, its explorers had to turn to other countries for financial support.
   (3) Although India was Columbus's original destination, Europeans lost interest in exploring the Orient.
   (4) Although religious persecution had been a problem, by the Age of Exploration there was generally religious tolerance.
   (5) Although the late 1400s was a period of exploration and discovery, it was also a time when art flourished.

3. The routes of the early European explorers best explain which of the following?

   (1) the later colonization patterns
   (2) why so many Europeans went to sea
   (3) how New York and Miami got their names
   (4) why the official language in the United States is English
   (5) why the Panama Canal was built

4. Which of the following best explains why the Americas were not named after either Columbus or Cabot?

   (1) Neither explorer was well-known.
   (2) Neither explorer had really reached the mainland.
   (3) Spain claimed the right to name the new lands.
   (4) Both sailors were more interested in wealth than in fame.
   (5) Vespucci brought home the first evidence of the New World's wealth.

Questions 5 through 7 refer to the following passage.

The thirteen original English colonies were established by corporations, like today's joint stock companies, or by proprietary agencies of one or more people. All received grants of territory from the English Crown. The members of these groups were motivated by interests in profiting from trade, extending English power, converting the Native Americans to Christianity, and pursuing religious freedom for oppressed sects. Many were also motivated to provide a new start for the poor and destitute, thus easing the burden on English workhouses and debtors' prisons.

5. Which of the following was a reason for colonization?

   (1) establishing a church-run estate
   (2) establishing a penal colony
   (3) making money
   (4) rebelling against England
   (5) establishing a democracy

6. According to the passage, why might some English citizens have become indentured servants to established colonials, thus giving up their freedom for up to seven years in exchange for passage and land of their own after their indenture was over?

   (1) Many of these people were running from the law.
   (2) They could not otherwise afford to make a new life in the Americas.
   (3) Their religious principles required them to humble themselves.
   (4) They were used to being servants in England.
   (5) They were misled by false promises from the corporations.

7. Widespread and systematic colonization was made possible by which of the following, according to the passage?

   (1) because life in England was intolerable
   (2) by grants of land subject to the English Crown
   (3) because of improved ocean navigation
   (4) by the abundance of natural resources in the Americas
   (5) because people recognized the importance of religious tolerance

Questions 8 through 11 refer to the following passage.

These famous words from *The Declaration of Independence,* ". . . Governments are instituted among Men, deriving their just powers from the consent of the governed, . . . whenever any Form of Government becomes destructive of these ends, it is the Right of the People to alter or abolish it. . . ." are based on the ideas of John Locke, an English philosopher of the seventeenth century. Locke wrote the following:

"There is therefore . . . another way whereby governments are dissolved, and that is when the legislative or the prince, either of them, act contrary to their trust. First, the legislative acts against the trust reposed in them when they endeavor to invade the property of the subject, and to make themselves or any part of the community masters or arbitrary disposers of the lives, liberties, or fortunes of the people.

"For the people having reserved to themselves the choice of their representatives as the fence to their properties, could do it for no other end but that they might always be freely chosen, freely act and advise as the necessity of the commonwealth and the public good should upon examination and mature debate be judged to require."

8. According to the passage, Locke believed which of the following?

   (1) Legislators can dissolve governments.
   (2) People have the right to privacy of property.
   (3) Governments do not have an obligation to their people.
   (4) People should have no say in who represents them.
   (5) Government representatives are responsible for property line fences.

9. Locke <u>most likely</u> would have supported which of the following?

   (1) colonists who objected to having to house British troops
   (2) the British government violating a treaty with the Ottawa
   (3) a group of angry colonists who raided a band of Native Americans who had converted to Christianity
   (4) Prime Minister Grenville who decided to tax American colonists to help repay debts from the Seven Years War
   (5) France when it ceded its North American holdings to Britain

10. Which of the following expressions best represents the American colonists' adoption of Locke's principles?

    (1) Give me liberty or give me death.
    (2) No taxation without representation.
    (3) I have not yet begun to fight.
    (4) The British are coming!
    (5) Join or die.

11. Which of the following explains why John Locke would have disagreed with the view that King George III deserved the American Revolution because he was feeble-minded?

    (1) The argument attacks the person rather than the issue of a violation of rights.
    (2) A king can govern well even if he is mentally ill.
    (3) The statement is not proof that King George was feeble-minded.
    (4) No king deserves rebellion of his subjects.
    (5) King George deserved sympathy.

Questions 12 through 14 refer to the following graph.

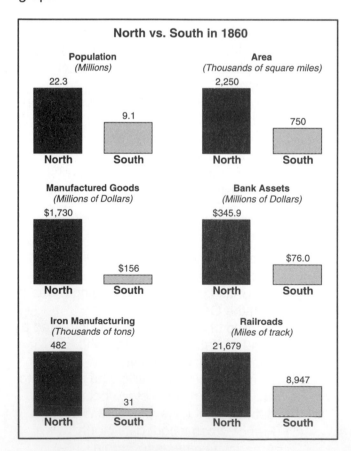

North vs. South in 1860

Population (Millions)
North 22.3   South 9.1

Area (Thousands of square miles)
North 2,250   South 750

Manufactured Goods (Millions of Dollars)
North $1,730   South $156

Bank Assets (Millions of Dollars)
North $345.9   South $76.0

Iron Manufacturing (Thousands of tons)
North 482   South 31

Railroads (Miles of track)
North 21,679   South 8,947

12. Which of the following was true of the North before the Civil War, according to the graph?

    (1) It had more slaves than the South.
    (2) It covered less territory than the South.
    (3) It had a more experienced government.
    (4) It had greater resources and labor forces than the South.
    (5) It was more committed to winning the war than was the South.

13. Based on information in the graph, which of the following statements is most justified?

    (1) It was through sheer determination on the part of the South that the war lasted four years.
    (2) Confederate leaders had no business conducting a war.
    (3) The North won because of moral superiority.
    (4) Slavery was not of economic benefit to the South.
    (5) An agrarian economy had no chance against an industrial economy.

14. Which of the following problems faced by the South during the Civil War can be concluded from information shown in the graph?

    (1) Part of Virginia split off and became West Virginia, joining the North.
    (2) Because of their opposition to slavery, European countries tended to favor the North.
    (3) The South had to spend money it desperately needed buying manufactured products from Europe.
    (4) Southern slaves, aspiring to freedom, sympathized with and even aided the North.
    (5) The North maintained control of the Navy.

Questions 15 through 17 refer to the following graph.

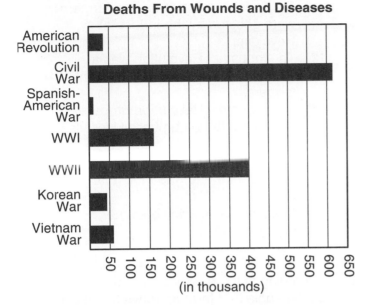

Deaths From Wounds and Diseases

(in thousands)

15. Based on the figures in the graph, which of the following **best** describes the Civil War?

    (1) the war between the states
    (2) a well-fought war
    (3) a major American tragedy
    (4) a waste of time and money
    (5) a good example for North and South Vietnam

16. The losses on both sides in the Civil War were especially hard for the nation to bear because of which of the following?

    (1) neither side had enough soldiers
    (2) friends and relatives were often among the enemy dead
    (3) the abolition of slavery would have happened anyway
    (4) the nation was in need of better soldiers
    (5) the national birthrate had decreased

17. Which of the following was **most likely** one of the major effects of the loss of life during the Civil War?

    (1) a serious shortage of workers
    (2) a destruction of agricultural land
    (3) an increase in banking transactions
    (4) a surge of industrial growth
    (5) the emergence of carpetbaggers

18. Which of the following statements about the Civil War is an opinion rather than a fact?

    (1) The North had a larger population and more resources.
    (2) Ironclad ships were used for the first time in the Civil War.
    (3) Lacking sufficient numbers of volunteers, both the North and the South passed draft laws.
    (4) After the Civil War, Southern states passed "black codes," designed to deprive blacks of certain basic rights.
    (5) Northern victory in the Civil War ensured the emergence of the United States as a world power.

Question 19 refers to the following passage from Abraham Lincoln's Inaugural Address, March 4, 1861.

. . . I hold that, in contemplation of universal law and of the Constitution, the union of these states is perpetual. Perpetuity is implied, if not expressed, in the fundamental law of all national governments. It is safe to assert that no government proper ever had a provision in its organic law for its own termination. Continue to execute all the express provisions of our national Constitution, and the Union will endure forever—it being impossible to destroy it except by some action not provided for in the instrument itself. . . .

19. Which of the following **best** explains the probable purpose of the passage?

    (1) to free the slaves
    (2) to win the civil war
    (3) to abolish free trade
    (4) to discourage secession of states
    (5) to ensure Lincoln's reelection

Questions 20 through 24 refer to the following passage.

One of the first effects of the Industrial Revolution in America was on the lifestyles of craftspeople and farmers. Finding themselves in competition with machinery that could produce the same products more quickly and for lower prices, many craftspeople gave up their traditional work and turned to full-time farming. Some in rural areas moved to the cities to work in factories where their skills could be used. Still others turned to occupations that were related to their former crafts. For example, some cabinetmakers, who had often doubled as undertakers because they made the coffins, became full-time undertakers. Still others became innkeepers because they had a ready supply of furniture and maintenance skills.

The production of factory goods also affected farmers who had relied on the barter system for obtaining the items they could not make or grow themselves. Because they were no longer able to trade easily for what they needed, many farmers changed to cash-crop farming. This change often involved a need for more land. While self-sufficient farmers needed only enough land to grow food for their families and for trading purposes, cash-crop farmers had to grow enough to sell. The more land one had, the more cash one had. Cash-crop farmers also needed hired hands to help work the land and to run the machinery in order to farm the larger acreage. Some farmers finally moved to the cities because they couldn't raise or sell enough crops to survive.

20. Which of the following twentieth-century farming trends in the United States occurred many years after the Industrial Revolution?

   (1) increased farm size
   (2) decreased number of farms
   (3) increased mechanization
   (4) emphasis on selling crops for cash rather than growing only enough food to feed one's family
   (5) development of agricultural cooperatives to handle and sell products

21. Which conclusion may be drawn from the passage?

   (1) Only a few craftspeople and farmers were affected by the Industrial Revolution.
   (2) The Industrial Revolution was a welcome change for self-sufficient farmers.
   (3) The Industrial Revolution probably changed a large number of lifestyles in America.
   (4) The occupation of undertaker became very popular after the Industrial Revolution.
   (5) City factories quickly became overcrowded.

22. According to the passage, why did some craftspeople and farmers move to the cities?

   (1) They had grown tired of country life.
   (2) Food was more plentiful in the cities.
   (3) Living in the country was hard work.
   (4) They were looking for jobs.
   (5) Factory goods were more available in the cities.

23. Which of the following is an assumption, rather than a fact, presented in the passage?

   (1) A number of farms increased their acreage.
   (2) Factory goods were cheaper than goods made by traditional craftspeople.
   (3) Factory jobs were available in the cities.
   (4) Some people had to find different occupations.
   (5) All self-sufficient farmers had to become cash-crop farmers.

24. Which of the following twentieth-century inventions would have effects most similar to those of the Industrial Revolution?

   (1) the microwave oven
   (2) the cellular telephone
   (3) computer technology
   (4) cable television
   (5) the jet propulsion engine

Question 25 refers to the following graph.

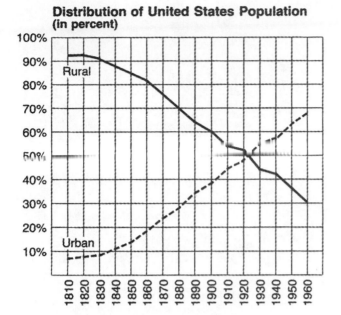

Distribution of United States Population (in percent)

25. Which of the following statements is best supported by the information in this graph?

    (1) European immigrants were pouring into American cities before the turn of the century.
    (2) Large-scale agribusinesses were responsible for driving people from their farms.
    (3) Within one century, the American economy shifted from being primarily agrarian to a more industrial economy.
    (4) People began leaving the cities after the turn of the century.
    (5) The distribution of the United States population reached a balance in 1900.

Questions 26 through 28 refer to the following passage.

Traditionally, cities and city governments were small, and power was divided among various branches. In the late nineteenth century, the populations and needs of American cities grew rapidly. This period saw the rise of the political machine. Political machines were groups that were usually associated with parties and were under the leadership of a boss. Machines helped city dwellers find things they desperately needed: jobs, housing, food, clothes, and medical care. These favors were a way to buy votes, for machine politicians were more interested in power than in the good of the people. They often resorted to bribery and graft.

26. Which of the following may have been a reason these corrupt organizations were called machines?

    (1) They were all very much alike.
    (2) They manufactured votes.
    (3) They were products of industrialization.
    (4) They were very powerful.
    (5) They helped to rebuild the cities.

27. Which of the following is most likely a direct cause of political machines?

    (1) the rebellion of city dwellers against established government practices
    (2) the growing number of services that cities had to provide
    (3) the development of modern methods of communication
    (4) the development of modern methods of transportation
    (5) the presence of strong mayors and city councils

28. Which of the statesments below could have been a reason illegal businesses such as gambling and prostitution benefited from political machines?

    (1) The politicians ignored them.
    (2) The politicians were uninterested in law enforcement.
    (3) The businesses could pay corrupt politicians to leave them alone.
    (4) The politicians were the ones who ran those businesses.
    (5) The police were too busy investigating the politicians.

SIGHTSEEING IN 1920

The caption on this 1920 cartoon from *Life* reads as follows: "That depression down there is where New York City stood. But with all its skyscrapers and underground tunnels it suddenly sunk one day and they haven't been able to find it since."

29. According to the cartoon, what is the major cause for the disappearance of New York City?

   (1) an earthquake
   (2) the skyscrapers were too high
   (3) the land could no longer support its weight
   (4) too many people lived there
   (5) it had become an underground city

30. What opinion is the cartoonist expressing?

   (1) growth of a city is not always good
   (2) people in 1920 will enjoy sightseeing
   (3) American cities are health hazards
   (4) the buildings in New York City are poorly constructed
   (5) balloon flights are popular tourist attractions

THE PROGRESS OF ART

31. Which of the following is the best alternative title for this cartoon from the early 1900s?

   (1) Too Much a Sign of the Times
   (2) How To Get the Most Out of an Ad
   (3) Strange Foods of the City
   (4) The Most Effective Use of Art
   (5) The Growth of American Business

32. What does the bag in the cartoon most likely represent?

   (1) improvements in advertising
   (2) the increased cost of building in the city
   (3) the money involved in advertising
   (4) the results of eating brain food
   (5) a rejection of old-fashioned art

33. Based on the information in the cartoon, which choice best describes how the cartoonist sees advertising?

As

   (1) a blight on the urban landscape
   (2) a burden to women
   (3) a good source of information
   (4) a source of employment for artists
   (5) the economic foundation of cities

Questions 34 through 36 refer to the following passage and table.

Before World War II, women workers were not welcome in industrial jobs. But wartime labor shortages brought 2.5 million women to the factories. Many of these women, who were married and over thirty-five, became welders, toolmakers, and blast furnace operators.

Women in the Civilian Labor Force, 1900–1998

Year	Number (thousands)	% Female population aged 16 and over	% of labor force population aged 16 and over
1900	5,319	18.8%	18.3%
1910	7,445	21.5	19.9
1920	8,637	21.4	20.4
1930	10,752	22.0	22.0
1940	12,845	25.4	24.3
1950	18, 389	33.9	29.6
1960	23,240	37.7	33.4
1970	31,543	43.3	38.1
1980	45,487	51.5	42.5
1990	56,829	57.5	45.2
1993	58,795	57.9	45.5
1994	60,239	58.8	46.0
1996	61,857	59.3	46.2
1997	63,036	59.8	46.2
1998	63,714	59.8	46.3

34. The importance of the role these women played is best expressed in which of the following?

   (1) in the phrase "Rosie the riveter"
   (2) in the phrase "a woman's place is in the home"
   (3) in the phrase "woman's work is never done"
   (4) in the phrase "keep the home fires burning"
   (5) by the actions of ax-wielding Carry Nation

35. Which of the following reasons best indicates why women who stayed in manufacturing in 1945 were dissatisfied when they were paid 65% of what men earned for the same job?

   (1) Women had gotten used to better wages.
   (2) The men performed the jobs better.
   (3) Women had already proved that they could do the jobs.
   (4) Women did not want to work in the home.
   (5) Women wanted to be housewives.

36. Which of the following statements is supported by the information in the table?

   (1) Women made up most of the civilian labor force in 1940.
   (2) Women have participated in the civilian labor force in increasing numbers.
   (3) Men were outnumbered by women in the civilian workforce in 1950.
   (4) Few women participated in the civilian workforce in 1940.
   (5) The 20th century saw decreasing participation of women in the workforce.

Question 37 refers to the following cartoon.

Rob Rodgers reprinted by permission of United Feature Syndicate, Inc.

37. The boy wearing dark glasses is most likely which of the following?

   (1) a delinquent student
   (2) a student interested in literature
   (3) a music student
   (4) a student with poor math skills
   (5) an excellent student

Questions 38 through 41 refer to the following passage.

The decade from 1960 to 1969 will be remembered by many as a period of social and political unrest in the United States. During this time, many people despaired over the clothing worn and the music listened to by American youth. However, that music was often a sign of the times and a reflection of the tensions and changes that were affecting much of American society. In the early sixties, questions about social justice were raised by songs such as Bob Dylan's "Blowin' in the Wind" and "The Chimes of Freedom Flashing" which echoed the civil rights song "We Shall Overcome." But at the same time, the Beach Boys were singing about school spirit and fun in the sun. The early conflict about military involvement in Vietnam was sung about in 1965 by Barry McGuire in the discouraging song "Eve of Destruction" and by Barry Sadler in the patriotic song "Ballad of the Green Beret." A few years later, a gradual shift in mood became evident in Dylan's song "John Wesley Harding" which suggested calmer questions and possible answers even as Country Joe and the Fish protested loudly against the draft. Finally, music as a mirror of the political and social process in America was highlighted at Woodstock, New York, where half a million young people came together in 1969 to spend three days listening to songs that spanned the decade. This event, like John Lennon's public performance of "Give Peace a Chance" in November 1969, was a symbol of the desire for unity within a time of turmoil. Woodstock was a display of hope in days of rage.

38. Which of the following conclusions can be drawn from this passage?

What we view as historical events are

(1) not simply isolated names and dates
(2) ignored by young people
(3) subjects of controversy
(4) highly symbolic
(5) really symptoms of larger cycles

39. According to this passage, how might much of the music of the sixties be regarded?

As

(1) a symptom of political apathy
(2) empty-headed rebellion
(3) a reaffirmation of some American ideals
(4) harmful to moral and physical health
(5) a return to normalcy

40. In addition to reflecting social and political values, the music of the sixties most likely

(1) influenced the values of American youth
(2) brought the Vietnam conflict to an end
(3) created a generation of drug addicts
(4) showed adults the error of their ways
(5) returned to the concept of innocence

41. Which of the following does information in this passage indicate about the American youth of the sixties?

They were

(1) taking too many drugs
(2) politically aware
(3) self-absorbed
(4) against the Vietnam War
(5) uninterested in social issues

Question 42 refers to the following passage.

Shortly after World War II ended, the Cold War began. The Cold War refers to the hostility and struggle between the United States and its allies, and the Soviet Union and its allies. Each side feared expansion by the other and prepared to prevent such expansion. The Cold War ended with the demise of the Soviet Union in 1991.

42. How would the end of the Cold War be most likely to affect the United States?

(1) decrease U.S. defense budgets
(2) lessen U.S. influence in the world
(3) improve U.S. balance of trade
(4) increase U.S. tax revenues
(5) increase U.S. interest in international, as opposed to domestic, issues

Questions 43 through 47 refer to the following passage.

It is all too easy to think of history as being about times that are dead and gone or as lists of names and dates. But the events that are recorded as America's history were the results of real people doing real things on a daily basis. What we call history is more than a written record of the past; it is the way people in the present view what has happened and what is happening now. Although our history consists of everything that everyone has done, historians highlight what seems most significant in terms of long-lasting effect.

It has been said that history repeats itself, that history is a continuous development from necessity to freedom, and that history is always written wrong and so must always be rewritten. Whichever view of history one may take, the important thing is to consider how the past, essentially yesterday's news, affects the actions of those people living in the present.

43. According to the passage, how would historians describe history?

(1) as random events
(2) from many points of view
(3) as unrelated events
(4) as unimportant
(5) as a record of people's mistakes

44. What might the suggestion "no one was listening the first time" explain about history?

(1) It is about the past.
(2) It must be rewritten.
(3) It affects the modern world.
(4) It repeats itself.
(5) It is a continuous process.

45. A person says, "Oh, I knew about that a long time ago. That's yesterday's news." What does this comment suggest about the historical importance of today's events?

(1) They are less important than what happened yesterday.
(2) Historians are more interested in the present than the past.
(3) Current events eventually become part of the historical record.
(4) Reporters of today's news are the historians of tomorrow.
(5) Nothing that happens is really important.

46. A historian recently discovered some new information about the causes of the French Revolution. This new perspective would best be described as which of the following?

(1) a necessary element of freedom
(2) history being rewritten
(3) history repeating itself
(4) a record of people's mistakes
(5) arrival at the truth

47. Adlai Stevenson's comment, "We can chart our future clearly and wisely only when we know the path which has led to the present," is best supported by which of the following ideas suggested in the passage?

(1) One person's interpretation of actions and their consequences will probably be limited.
(2) Historians sometimes discover that other historians were wrong.
(3) History is more than names and dates.
(4) History is about people and not events.
(5) The past affects the lives of people in the present.

Question 48 refers to the following passage.

In the 1860 Presidential Election, Abraham Lincoln faced a disorganized and fractured Democratic party. A Democratic convention in Charleston had resulted not in unity, but in two separate Democratic candidates—John Breckenridge and Stephen A. Douglas. A third party, The Constitutional Union party, also participated in the election. So lacking in unity was the Democratic party that it went down in defeat to Lincoln, who won 180 electoral votes against 123 total electoral votes for his opponents.

48. Which of the following conclusions is supported by the passage?

(1) Lincoln won a decisive electoral victory.
(2) Slavery was not a major issue in the campaign.
(3) Stephen A. Douglas won more popular votes than his rival Democrat.
(4) Had Douglas not run, Breckenridge might have been elected.
(5) Lincoln's electoral votes indicated broad support across the country.

Questions 49 through 53 refer to the following passage.

When Franklin D. Roosevelt became President, the nation was still suffering from economic troubles. He created the New Deal by proposing legislation concerning federal economies, unemployment relief, and limits on stock buying. He created so many agencies that they were referred to by initials: NRA (National Recovery Administration), AAA (Agricultural Adjustment Administration), FERA (Federal Emergency Relief Administration), CCC (Civilian Conservation Corps), HOLC (Home Owners Loan Corporation), TVA (Tennessee Valley Authority), PWA (Public Works Administration), and WPA (Works Progress Administration). Many of the New Deal programs instituted a certain amount of government control over the financial actions of Americans. The CCC and the WPA created jobs for over nine million workers. The National Recovery Act (ruled unconstitutional in 1935) required businesses to set up rules for fair competition. Farmers were paid for not growing crops, thus raising the prices for their products. The Tennessee Valley Authority built dams that controlled floods and produced electricity. It also promoted wildlife preserves and conservation of natural resources. The Social Security Act was the federal insurance plan that required workers and employers to contribute to a retirement fund. These plans were fairly successful in aiding the nation's recovery, but most eventually ended because some people felt that government had become too powerful.

49. Which of the following implies freedom of choice for the governed?

   (1) regulation of business practices
   (2) interference in agriculture
   (3) production of electricity for the Tennessee Valley
   (4) mandatory worker contribution to Social Security
   (5) mandatory employer contribution to Social Security

50. Which of the following was an assumption about government and the capitalist economic system on which the New Deal was probably based?

   (1) Capitalism does not work, and the government should totally control the economy.
   (2) Capitalism works well, and the government should not interfere with it.
   (3) Capitalism has some problems, which the government should try to deal with through regulation.
   (4) Neither capitalism nor government can much affect the lives of ordinary people.
   (5) The main role of government should be to promote the capitalist system.

51. Which of the following was the main objective of the New Deal?

   (1) save human and natural resources
   (2) extend the power of the presidency
   (3) improve working conditions
   (4) halt unemployment
   (5) stop unethical business practices

52. Why might some people have given the lighthearted nickname of "alphabet soup" to the programs of the New Deal?

   (1) The programs were easy to memorize.
   (2) The programs were known by many initials.
   (3) None of the projects were successful.
   (4) The plans were regarded as childish.
   (5) The New Deal projects were intended for the health of the nation.

53. Which of the following facts from the passage might groups opposed to the New Deal have used in support of the argument that the programs were a drain on the federal budget?

   (1) Wildlife conservation was part of the TVA.
   (2) Social Security taxes were mandatory.
   (3) The NRA was ruled unconstitutional.
   (4) Millions of workers were paid by the government.
   (5) The prices of crops rose.

Questions 54 and 55 refer to the following passage and map.

In 2000, the contentious Presidential election between Al Gore and George Bush left many wondering about the validity of the electoral college: the Electoral College seemed to override the will of the people. Indeed, the current election was not without precedent. In 1888, the Electoral College favored Benjamin Harrison over Grover Cleveland, despite the fact that Cleveland (like Al Gore) won the popular vote. The Constitution provides for the selection of electors. Article II, Section I reads as follows, in part:

Each State shall appoint, in such manner as the Legislature thereof may direct, a number of electors, equal to the whole number of Senators and Representatives to which the State may be entitled in the Congress; but no Senator or Representative, or person holding office of trust or profit under the United States, shall be appointed an elector.

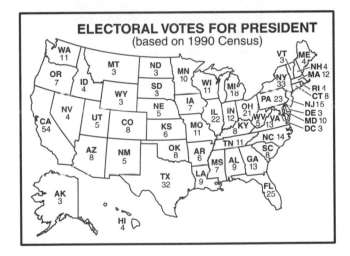

ELECTORAL VOTES FOR PRESIDENT
(based on 1990 Census)

54. Which of the following statements can be inferred from the passage?

(1) Benjamin Harrison found his support among Senators.
(2) Grover Cleveland, like Al Gore, won the popular vote but lost in the Electoral College.
(3) George Bush won most states.
(4) Benjamin Harrison won as many votes in the Electoral College as George Bush.
(5) Al Gore needed more support in Congress to win.

55. Of the following, which state has only one representative?

(1) Colorado
(2) Missouri
(3) Rhode Island
(4) Hawaii
(5) Alaska

Question 56 refers to the following table.

Enrollment in Public and Private Schools, 1899–2010

School Year[1]	Public school[2] enrollment	Private school[2] enrollment	% Private
1899–1900	15,503	1,352	8.7
1909–1910	17,814	1,558	8.7
1919–1920	21,578	1,699	7.9
1929–1930	25,678	2,651	10.3
1939–1940	25,434	2,611	10.3
1949–1950	25,111	3,380	13.5
1959–1960	35,182	5,675	16.1
1969–1970	45,500	5,500[3]	12.1
1979–1980	41,651	5,000[3]	12.0
1989–1990	40,543	5,355[3]	11.7
1999–2000[4]	46,812	5,938	11.3
2009–2010[4]	47,109	5,947	11.2

(1) Fall enrollment. (2) in thousands. (3) Estimated. (4) Projected

56. Which of the following statements best characterizes the trend in private school enrollment?

(1) It has declined as a percentage since 1960.
(2) It has grown steadily.
(3) It seems to peak at the end of a century.
(4) Most parents want to send their children to private schools.
(5) Children in 1900 were more likely to attend private schools than children in 1999.

Directions: Choose the <u>one best answer</u> to each question.

Question 1 refers to the following passage.

The Phoenicians, consummate traders who lived where Lebanon now exists, provided the world with its first systematic alphabet, consisting of twenty-two consonants. It was easy to use and quickly became a standard in international trade. The Greeks added vowels to create the first fully-formed written alphabet.

1. Which of the following conclusions is supported by the information in the passage?

   (1) The Greeks were smarter than the Phoenicians.
   (2) Phoenician traders transmitted their alphabet throughout the Mediterranean.
   (3) Alphabets are necessary for trade.
   (4) All writing requires vowels.
   (5) Phoenicians lived in isolation because of their location.

Questions 2 through 4 refer to the following passage.

At its height from the ninth through the fifteenth century A.D., the Khmer Empire extended well beyond the boundaries of present-day Cambodia. The Khmers were influenced by the eastern sweep of Indian culture. Nominally Buddhist, the Khmer people also retained earlier animist beliefs. The Khmer capital of Angkor, which today is considered one of the architectural wonders of the world, evinces the twin influences of Hindu and Buddhist architecture and embodies the grandiosity of the Khmer Empire. Under attack from neighboring Thailand, Angkor was sacked in 1431 and the capital moved to Phnom Penh. Only in the nineteenth century were the city and its temples rediscovered by French missionaries.

Angkor is the largest complex of architecture and sculpture ever created. It consists of shrines, cloisters, and temples linked by corridors and stairways. Enormous reservoirs and canals surround the huge stone structures built by the Khmer kings. Each king built successively larger structures. The largest, Angkor Wat, was nearly 5,000 feet by 5,000 feet. It was built by Suryavaram II, who ruled from 1113–1150.

2. Which of the following explains the importance of Angkor?

   (1) It is the largest religious complex ever created.
   (2) Its fall marked the end of the Khmer Empire.
   (3) Angkor fostered a new political philosophy.
   (4) It developed the first civil servants in the world.
   (5) Angkor became a primary site for terrorism in Asia.

3. What was the <u>most likely</u> use for the system of reservoirs and canals that formed part of the Angkor complex?

   (1) fishing
   (2) irrigation
   (3) swimming
   (4) boating
   (5) water skiing

4. Which of the following is the <u>most likely</u> purpose of the monuments of Angkor?

   (1) to defend against Indian incursion
   (2) to house common people
   (3) to demonstrate imperial power
   (4) to give artists jobs
   (5) to rival the Gothic cathedrals of Europe

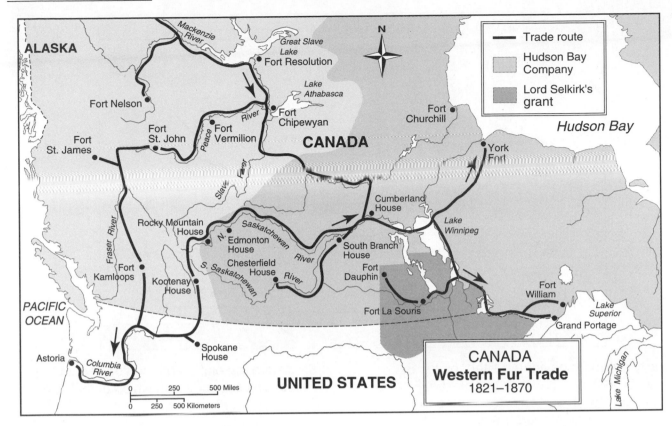

The Hudson Bay Company, an English trading company, played a major role in the settlement of Canada. Established in 1671, the company operated primarily in the Hudson and James Bays. In the late eighteenth century, a federation of independent fur traders formed the North West Company, galvanizing Hudson Bay into expansion. Lord Selkirk, who controlled Hudson Bay, established the Red River Settlement as an off-shoot of Hudson Bay. The rivalry between Hudson Bay and North West degenerated into armed conflict and lengthy litigation. The companies merged in 1821, by which time the fur trade reached beyond Hudson Bay's original limits. The Canadian government purchased much land in central Canada from Hudson Bay in 1869. The company continued to flourish, moving from furs into real estate and oil and gas production.

5. Which of the following is the most likely reason for Hudson Bay's expansion?

   (1) depletion of beavers
   (2) increased competition
   (3) redrawing of its limits
   (4) increased demand
   (5) assistance from Lord Selkirk

6. Which of the following is the most likely reason that Cumberland House was located at the confluence of two rivers?

   To

   (1) obtain fresh water
   (2) take advantage of the favorable climate
   (3) facilitate transportation of fur
   (4) facilitate settlement of traders
   (5) stop competition from the North West Company

7. Which of the following conclusions is supported by information in the passage and the map?

   (1) The fur trade was immoral.
   (2) Native Americans participated in the fur trade.
   (3) The North West Company was exclusively British.
   (4) The fur trade reached across territorial limits.
   (5) Conflicts arose because courts did not have sufficient jurisdiction over trade.

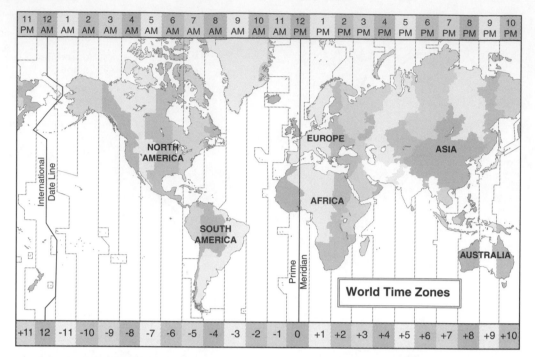

Early mariners navigated either by local knowledge of landmarks or by celestial reckoning. However, sea travel during the Renaissance heightened the demand for systematic navigational methods. To navigate properly, mariners needed to know their precise location. To find latitude, Portuguese navigators used the Pole Star for measuring the distance from the equator in the Northern Hemisphere and solar declination tables for figuring latitude in the Southern Hemisphere.

Longitude—the east-west measure—was far more difficult to master. In the mid-1700s, British inventors developed the mariner's sextant, which helped determine longitudinal position by measuring the angle from the horizon to the moon. For more precise measurements, however, an excellent timepiece was needed. Responding to a call from the British Board of Longitude, John Harrison, a clockmaker, set to work developing a chronometer. After decades of experimentation, he submitted a prototype in 1762. As chronometers became cheaper and more reliable, the lunar method of determining longitude became outmoded.

The standard measurement of longitude from Greenwich, England as a starting point also determined the structure of time zones, established formally in 1884.

8. Before the eighteenth century, seagoing vessels depended on which of the following to navigate?

(1) trade winds
(2) the stars
(3) sea depths
(4) longitude
(5) sonar

9. According to the passage, which of the following made the determination of international time zones possible?

(1) mariner's sextant
(2) compass
(3) gyroscope
(4) chronometer
(5) barometer

10. Before the 1884 formalization of time zones, localities determined their own times. Railroad transportation benefited greatly from establishing formal boundary lines. Which of the following is the most likely explanation for this benefit?

(1) With time zones, engineers wouldn't have to use sextants.
(2) Time zones sped up the clock.
(3) Time zones regularized schedules across local and national lines.
(4) Passengers could ignore local time.
(5) Time zones extended daylight hours.

11. Which of the following was most likely a factor in determining the placement of the Prime Meridian?

   (1) the location of the Royal Greenwich Observatory near London
   (2) the importance of New York as a port
   (3) the fact that Australia is near the International Date Line
   (4) the proximity of the Mediterranean Sea
   (5) the importance of Iceland in the history of navigation

Question 12 refers to the following passage.

In 1861, under Alexander II, serfdom, the feudal system that had virtually enslaved Russian peasants since the Middle Ages, was abolished. However, the emancipation took place slowly and peasants were taxed heavily for any land they were given. As a result, they remained economically tied to their villages.

12. What effect might the system of serfdom have had on Russia's industrialization?

   (1) It hastened industrialization by ensuring free labor.
   (2) It slowed industrialization by tying former serfs to rural lives.
   (3) It encouraged industrialization by moving serfs into the middle class.
   (4) It enabled rapid industrialization by exiling serfs to rural Russia.
   (5) It discouraged industrialization by lowering taxes.

Questions 13 and 14 refer to the following passage.

Railroads played a major role in the Industrial Revolution from the nineteenth century through the mid-twentieth. By the first part of the twentieth century, nearly 900,000 miles of railways existed. Almost every nation had some form of rail transport. Toward the end of the twentieth century, railroad mileage was about 800,000 miles.

13. According to the passage, railroads were first successful in which of the following?

   (1) industrial countries
   (2) agricultural communities
   (3) mountainous terrain
   (4) semi-nomadic regions
   (5) coastal sections

14. Which of the following conclusions can be drawn from the information in the passage?

   (1) Railroad usage was increasing at the end of the twentieth century.
   (2) Railroad travel was declining at the end of the twentieth century.
   (3) Airplane travel was increasing in the twentieth century.
   (4) Automobile travel replaced rail travel in the twentieth century.
   (5) Steamships were replacing railroads by the end of the twentieth century.

Question 15 refers to the following information.

China: Wars of Resistance	
1839–1842	Anglo-Chinese (Opium) War
1856–1860	Anglo-French War
1894–1895	Sino-Japanese War
1898–1900	Boxer Rebellion (against the British)
1911–1912	Rebellion and the End of Chinese Monarchy

15. From the information in the chart, which of the following conclusions can be drawn about nineteenth century China?

   It was

   (1) essentially independent
   (2) totally democratic
   (3) completely isolated
   (4) dominated by foreign interests
   (5) flourishing under foreign protection

Questions 16 through 20 refer to the following tables.

Allied Losses World War I*

Country	Total # Soldiers	Dead in Battle	Civilians Dead	Financial Cost in $ Millions
Russia	12,000,000	1,700,000	2,000,000	25,600
U.K.	8,904,467	908,371	30,633	51,975
France	8,410,000	1,357,800	40,000	49,877
Italy	5,615,000	462,391	0**	18,143
U.S.	4,355,000	50,585	0**	32,320
Japan	800,000	300	0**	0**
Romania	750,000	334,706	275,000	2,601
Serbia	707,343	45,000	650,000	2,400
Belgium	267,000	513,715	30,000	10,195
Greece	230,000	5,000	132,000	556
Portugal	100,000	100,000	0**	0**
Montenegro	50,000	3,000	0**	2,400

*All figures approximate.
**Figures not available

Central Powers Losses World War I*

Country	Total # Soldiers	Dead in Battle	Civilians Dead	Financial Cost in $ Millions
Germany	7,800,000	1,808,546	760,000	58,027
Austria-Hungary	7,800,000	922,500	300,000	23,706
Turkey	2,850,000	325,000	2,150,000	3,445
Bulgaria	1,200,000	75,844	275,000	1,015

*All figures approximate.

Total Losses World War I*

	Total # Soldiers	Dead in Battle	Civilians Dead	Financial Cost in $ Millions
Total Central Powers	19,650,000	3,131,889	3,485,000	86,238
Total Allied	42,188,810	4,888,891	3,157,633	193,367

*All figures approximate.

16. Which information in the tables supports the generalization that in the twentieth century, wars increasingly became a deadlier enterprise for civilians than for fighting men?

    (1) a comparison of soldiers mobilized to citizens dead
    (2) a comparison of citizens dead to financial costs
    (3) a comparison of total soldiers killed on both sides to total civilians dead
    (4) a comparison of French soldiers killed to French civilians killed
    (5) a comparison of allied civilians killed to central powers civilians killed

17. Which of these countries lost the greatest percentage of its soldiers?

    (1) Germany
    (2) Russia
    (3) France
    (4) Portugal
    (5) Romania

18. In which of the following countries did more civilians die than soldiers?

    (1) Romania
    (2) Greece
    (3) France
    (4) Germany
    (5) United Kingdom (U.K.)

19. With trench warfare a predominant strategy of WWI, which of the following inventions was most likely a major factor in the deaths of soldiers?

    (1) long-range bombers
    (2) machine guns
    (3) vaccines
    (4) dirigibles
    (5) submarines

20. Which of the following countries bore the greatest financial cost?

    (1) Russia
    (2) U.K.
    (3) France
    (4) Germany
    (5) U.S.

Questions 21 through 24 refer to the following map.

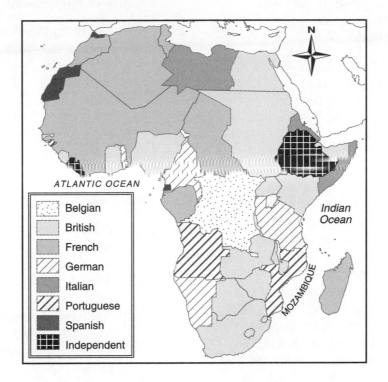

21. Which of the following statements is supported by the map?

   (1) Germany did not establish territories in Africa.
   (2) Italy and Portugal were colonial rivals.
   (3) Portugal established colonial territories mainly in north Africa.
   (4) Britain and France annexed the majority of African territory.
   (5) Spain annexed more African territory than Portugal.

22. Although Portugal had been a colonial power in Africa since the fifteenth century, corruption and poor management reduced Portugal's holdings to Angola and Mozambique, both of which became free in 1975.

   Which was the most likely reason for Portugal's decline in Africa?

   (1) civil war at home
   (2) economic depression abroad
   (3) crop failure in the colonies
   (4) inefficiency in colonial matters
   (5) preoccupation with European affairs

23. Which of the following colonial powers had a colony with no seaport?

   (1) Belgium
   (2) Italy
   (3) Britain
   (4) France
   (5) Spain

24. Which of the following is a conclusion supported by the information?

   (1) Colonialism waned in the twentieth century.
   (2) Africa escaped most colonialism.
   (3) Without WWII, Africa would still be colonized.
   (4) The Congo suffered the most.
   (5) Colonialism follows mercantilism.

Questions 25 through 29 refer to the following passage from a speech given in the United States by Jawaharlal Nehru, Prime Minister of India, December 18, 1956.

"The preservation of peace forms the central aim of India's policy. It is in the pursuit of this policy that we have chosen the path of nonalignment in any military or like pact of alliance. Nonalignment does not mean passivity of mind or action, lack of faith or conviction. It does not mean submission to what we consider evil. It is a positive and dynamic approach to such problems that confront us. We believe that each country has not only the right to freedom but also to decide its own policy and way of life. Only thus can true freedom flourish and a people grow according to their own genius.

We believe, therefore, in nonaggression and non-interference by one country in the affairs of another and the growth of tolerance between them and the capacity for peaceful coexistence. We think that by the free exchange of ideas and trade and other contacts between nations each will learn from the other and truth will prevail. We therefore endeavor to maintain friendly relations with all countries, even though we may disagree with them in their policies or structure of government. We think that by this approach we can serve not only our country but also the larger causes of peace and good fellowship in the world."

Nehru was long active in the struggle against the British for Indian independence and became India's first head of state after freedom was achieved. During the Cold War, he was a strict adherent to neutrality and refused to align India with either the USSR or the United States.

25. Nehru's speech is designed to win acceptance for which of the following concepts?

   (1) neutrality in the Cold War
   (2) antagonism toward tyrannies
   (3) belief in social democracy
   (4) neutrality in relation to Pakistan
   (5) rejection of colonialism

26. Based on the beliefs stated in the passage, which of the following would Nehru favor?

   (1) war of aggression
   (2) student exchanges
   (3) high tariffs
   (4) interference in United States domestic affairs
   (5) invasion of Sweden's air space by planes from another country

27. Which of the following conclusions could be drawn from the passage?

   (1) India refused to trade with Great Britain.
   (2) Nehru declined to address U.S. manufacturers.
   (3) African business leaders were not welcome in India.
   (4) Nehru would be willing to open trade negotiations with the Soviet Union.
   (5) French artists would be banned from India.

28. To what experience in Indian history might Nehru have been alluding when he used the words "each country has ... the right to freedom"?

   (1) World War II
   (2) the Gupta Dynasty
   (3) independence from Britain
   (4) the struggle with Pakistan
   (5) the assassination of Gandhi

29. Which of the following is the most likely reason that Nehru gave the nonalignment speech in the United States?

   (1) Everyone reads U.S. newspapers.
   (2) He wanted to justify India's position of nonalignment to the U.S.
   (3) He was never invited to the USSR.
   (4) He could give the speech in English.
   (5) Nonalignment involved only the U.S.

Question 30 refers to the following cartoon.

Highest Mission

30. What is suggested about democracy in the cartoon?

(1) It cannot flourish without arms.
(2) It must be protected.
(3) The UN walks away from democracies.
(4) Democracies need water.
(5) Democracies are agrarian-based systems.

Question 31 refers to the following passage.

In 1980, after the death of Marshall Tito, Communist Yugoslavia began to splinter. Bosnia declared independence in 1991. Unlike the other splinter states, which consisted of homogeneous ethnic groups, Bosnia contained Muslims, Serbs, and Croats. The neighboring Serb and Croatian states laid claim to parts of Bosnia. The result: war that only nominally ended with 1995 peace accords.

31. What is the most likely cause of Yugoslavian instability?

(1) differences among ethnic groups
(2) the resistance to capitalism
(3) Western European interference
(4) the breakup of the Soviet state
(5) World War II reparations

Question 32 refers to the following photograph.

32. This photograph from 1988 was taken in Tiananmen Square in Beijing during demonstrations to protest government policies in China. To the man on the street, what do the tanks probably represent?

(1) defense of the nation
(2) opposition to democracy
(3) national glory
(4) the media
(5) education

Directions: Choose the one best answer to each question.

Questions 1 through 3 refer to the following passage.

Each of us is a specialist in just a few areas of life; we are mechanics, farmers, teachers, homemakers, whatever. As a result we must depend on specialists in other economic areas for most of the goods and services we need.

To ensure that we will not be endangered by that dependency, we turn to government. Why endangered? Because almost all the specialists on whom we depend have no moral or legal obligation to us, aside from whatever they voluntarily assume or government requires. Primarily, they relate to us in an impersonal way, through money and profit. People who are bound by feelings of affection or friendship are most likely to treat each other fairly and honestly. A producer who never sees the consumer is less likely to be concerned about the individual who buys or uses his products. In this impersonal economic world in which we live, the drive to achieve success, measured by money or prestige, leads some individuals to ignore the safety and health needs of those who depend on them for goods and services. Not all producers, manufacturers, or service providers are irresponsible, of course, but enough of them are to make life sufficiently uncertain and dangerous for the rest of us, were it not for government.

1. Which of the following statements best represents the main idea of the passage?

    (1) Dependency on others makes people dependent on government.
    (2) People cannot depend on government.
    (3) Greed outweighs honesty.
    (4) Many products are dangerous.
    (5) There is no need for government regulation.

2. How does the government ensure the protection of its citizens?

    (1) by passing laws
    (2) by issuing press releases
    (3) through proclamations
    (4) with investigating committees
    (5) by conducting surveys

3. According to the passage, what is a primary function of government?

    (1) to guarantee liberty
    (2) to take care of the farmers
    (3) to make sure individuals are not too dependent on others
    (4) to ensure that producers can make as much profit as they want
    (5) to impose economic order on society

Question 4 refers to the following chart.

Political Divisions of the Senate, 1983–2003

Congress	Years	Democrats	Republicans
98th	1983–85	46	54
99th	1985–87	47	53
100th	1987–89	55	45
101st	1989–91	55	45
102nd	1991–93	56	44
103rd	1993–95	57	43
104th	1995–97	48	52
105th	1997–99	45	55
106th	1999–2001	45	55
107th	2001–03	50	50

4. Which of the following statements is supported by the chart?

    (1) The Senate has been under Republican rule for most of the last two decades.
    (2) The Democrats have been in the majority for the last two decades.
    (3) At no time in the last two decades has the House been under Republican rule.
    (4) The Senate fell under Republican rule in the 100th congress.
    (5) The Senate is currently under Democratic rule.

Questions 5 through 8 refer to the following passage.

The theory of democracy is based on four principles. First, every individual has value. Second, all individuals are entitled to freedom of choice. Third, there is no absolute truth. Fourth, all individuals are equal.

5. What does the statement that all individuals are equal mean?

    (1) Everyone has the same abilities.
    (2) All people should be given the same respect.
    (3) Given equal opportunities, all individuals can achieve the same goals.
    (4) People with disabilities should not be given special concessions.
    (5) People want the same things.

6. According to the passage, on what does the idea of democracy rest?

    (1) proven facts
    (2) firm ground
    (3) a set of beliefs
    (4) inalienable rights
    (5) self-evident truths

7. According to these principles of democracy, which of the following would be true?

    People should be able to

    (1) do whatever seems best at the time
    (2) discriminate against someone different from themselves
    (3) impose their beliefs on others
    (4) question the validity of a law
    (5) prohibit the general use of something they don't like

8. According to the passage, what would a person who values democracy do?

    (1) require candidates to use their own funds to run for office
    (2) encourage a friend to vote even though the friend favors another candidate
    (3) require a person running for office to have a college degree
    (4) favor lifetime service for lawmakers
    (5) keep some people from voting

Question 9 refers to the following cartoon.

9. Which of the following statements best summarizes the cartoonist's opinion of political candidates?

    (1) They employ large support staffs.
    (2) None of them should hire gag writers.
    (3) They don't seem to be able to speak for themselves.
    (4) Their speeches don't always make much sense.
    (5) They should give more credit to the quality of their speechwriters.

Questions 10 through 12 refer to the following passage about the Sixth Amendment to the U.S. Constitution.

In all criminal prosecutions, the accused shall enjoy the right to a speedy and public trial by an impartial jury of the State and district wherein the crime shall have been committed, which district shall have been previously ascertained by law, and to be informed of the nature and cause of the accusation; to be confronted with the witnesses against him; to have compulsory process for obtaining witnesses in his favor, and to have the Assistance of Counsel for his defense.

10. For which of the following reasons is it more difficult to get an impartial jury today than it was when the amendment was written?

   (1) Modern society is more opinionated than the colonials were.
   (2) People today are a lot more streetwise.
   (3) The news media often publicize the details of a crime before it comes to trial.
   (4) People today know more about criminal psychology.
   (5) Juries are in a hurry to end the trial, and they make snap judgments.

11. What would be the best title for this amendment?

   (1) Liberty for All
   (2) To Bear False Witness
   (3) Prevention of Unfair Arrest
   (4) The Trial Process
   (5) A Fair Trial

12. What did the writers of this amendment most likely intend to provide against?

   (1) an indecisive jury
   (2) trial of an innocent person
   (3) unjust imprisonment
   (4) lengthy court proceedings
   (5) dull trials

Questions 13 and 14 refer to the following excerpt from President Bill Clinton's 1995 State of the Union address.

America is once again the world's strongest economic power: almost six million new jobs in the last two years, exports booming, inflation down, high-wage jobs are coming back. A record number of American entrepreneurs are living the American dream.

If we want to stay that way, those who work and lift our nation must have more of its benefits.

Today, too many of those people are being left out. They're working harder for less. They have less security, less income, less certainty that they can even afford a vacation, much less college for their kids or retirement for themselves.

We cannot let this continue. If we don't act, our economy will probably keep doing what it's been doing since about 1978, when the income growth began to go to those at the very top of our economic scale. And the people in the vast middle got very little growth and people who worked like crazy but were on the bottom then, fell even further and further behind in the years afterward, no matter how hard they worked.

13. As indicated by this speech, what did President Clinton think government should do?

   (1) create more jobs
   (2) give scholarships to anyone who wants to go to college
   (3) help middle-class Americans find better jobs
   (4) ensure that working Americans benefit from economic growth
   (5) bring back high-wage jobs

14. If President Clinton had given advice to a major U.S. company that wanted to cut costs, what would he most likely suggest?

   That the company

   (1) lay off as many workers as possible
   (2) freeze wages for everyone except top executives
   (3) manufacture its products in another country where wages are lower
   (4) ask a labor union to help organize workers
   (5) reward workers who come up with cost-saving ideas

Questions 15 and 16 are based on the following cartoon.

By permission of Mike Luckovich and Creators Syndicate, Inc.

15. Of the following choices, which best expresses the cartoonist's opinion?

   (1) Opinion polls are as important as votes.
   (2) The man did his patriotic duty.
   (3) Opinion polls are mistakenly regarded as important.
   (4) People who respond to polls will also vote.
   (5) Polls should take the place of voting.

16. Which of the following most likely represents what the cartoonist thinks?

   (1) Some Americans do not really understand the political process.
   (2) Americans always do their patriotic duty.
   (3) Opinion polls will elect a politician.
   (4) Opinion polls are worthless.
   (5) Patriots always respond to opinion polls.

17. The United States traditionally has operated on a two-party political system. Recently, however, third-party nominees have shown up on ballots in major elections. What does this situation suggest?

   (1) The political system is falling apart.
   (2) The third party will gain more support.
   (3) Not all voters are satisfied with the two major parties.
   (4) The two major parties will change their policies.
   (5) The ballot system is being abused.

18. A tobacco company sends paid agents to Washington, D.C. to lobby in Congress against raising taxes on cigarettes. What does this exemplify?

   (1) unfair trade
   (2) a pressure group at work
   (3) an attack against antismoking campaigns
   (4) unfair taxation
   (5) corruption in the legislature

Questions 19 and 20 are based on the following passage.

Though qualified U.S. citizens have long had the right to vote, many don't go to the polls. In 2000, 51.2% of the U.S. voting age population participated in electing public representatives. Clearly many Americans did not vote. For citizens in a democratic country to participate in their local, state, and national government, they must vote. Voting is an effective way for the average citizen to exercise power. The idea of "one person, one vote" is the foundation of democracy.

19. According to the passage, which of the following statements represents the best reason to vote?

   (1) Your favorite candidate may lose if you don't vote.
   (2) Voting will give you a voice in how government is run.
   (3) The candidate you like least will win if you don't vote.
   (4) You will feel guilty if you don't vote.
   (5) The government will treat you unfairly if you don't vote.

20. Some people don't vote because they believe that their vote won't make a difference. How does this belief contradict the information in the passage?

   (1) It assumes that a large number of people will vote.
   (2) It suggests that the average voter doesn't understand the issues.
   (3) It goes against democratic principles.
   (4) It implies that all elections are rigged.
   (5) It assumes that the voter has unpopular ideas.

Questions 21 through 23 refer to the following definitions.

traditional authority—a power based on ancient custom, the claim to which is usually based on inheritance or birthright

legal-rational authority—a power granted by rules and laws that define the obligations of the officials

charismatic authority—a power that occurs because of the unique characteristics of a specific leader

21. Which of the following statements best explains why charismatic authority is an unstable basis for government?

    (1) Charismatic figures are unstable.
    (2) Power is centered on an individual who could fail or die.
    (3) The followers of a charismatic leader are fanatics.
    (4) Leaders with charismatic authority often head revolutions.
    (5) A personality-based authority will clash with a legal-rational authority.

22. Under which of the following systems would traditional authority be most likely to occur?

    (1) a democratic government
    (2) a socialist republic
    (3) a Communist state
    (4) a monarchy
    (5) a dictatorship

23. The definitions support the conclusion that in the U.S. an official's power comes from which of the following?

    (1) the office itself
    (2) personal characteristics
    (3) tradition
    (4) social status
    (5) loyal supporters

Questions 24 through 26 refer to the following passage.

In recent years U.S. politicians have generally been labeled as liberals or conservatives. Conservatives favor shrinking the size of government and cutting taxes. They tend to oppose government involvement in the economy and oppose most social welfare programs. Liberals, on the other hand, favor government playing a key role in economic and social issues. They feel that the government must provide a safety-net for its citizens.

Because many people share beliefs from both sides, it is often hard to identify a person as being liberal or conservative. Accordingly, conservatives and liberals sometimes agree on issues. For instance, they both favor shrinking the federal deficit. Yet they differ on how to go about it.

24. According to the passage, which of the following statements is a conservative most likely to make?

    (1) "Every worker should join a union."
    (2) "Less government regulation will help the economy."
    (3) "America doesn't need a strong defense."
    (4) "Raising taxes will help shrink the federal deficit."
    (5) "Government should play a greater role in people's lives."

25. The passage supports which of the following conclusions?

    (1) All liberals have the same beliefs.
    (2) Few conservatives favor cutting taxes.
    (3) Conservatives and liberals differ in their ideas about the role of government.
    (4) Conservatives and liberals can't agree on anything.
    (5) Liberals are pro-business.

26. The comparison between conservatives and liberals in this passage is generally based on which of the following?

    (1) different views on crime
    (2) their popularity with voters
    (3) their ability to change government
    (4) foreign policy issues
    (5) economic issues

Questions 27 through 30 refer to the following passage.

In seeking to lighten the President's burden, we would do well to recall the warning of Woodrow Wilson: "Men of ordinary physique and discretion cannot be Presidents and live, if the strain be not somehow relieved. We shall be obliged always to be picking our chief magistrates from among wise and prudent athletes—a small class." At the same time, we should also recall that a long list of routine tasks, each of which appears "nonessential" when viewed by itself, may well add up to an inspired performance of a great function of state. The President cannot be a successful Chief of State if he turns all the little ceremonies and visits over to the Vice President. He cannot lead Congress if he is unwilling to spend hours listening to Congressmen. And he cannot be a vigorous Commander in Chief unless he studies the defense budget item by item. For him as for all of us there is no final escape from hard and pedestrian labor. And as the gentlemen of Congress warned in the law of 1950 I have just mentioned: "Nothing contained herein shall relieve the President of his responsibility" for the acts of those "designated by him to perform functions." As Mr. Truman would say, the President may pass the details but not the buck.

27. The law of 1950 that the author refers to is most likely which of the following?

One that

(1) limits the responsibilities of the President
(2) adds more duties to the President
(3) allows the President to pass the buck
(4) permits the President to delegate some duties to aides
(5) relieves the President of all nonessential routine tasks

28. According to the initial quotation by Woodrow Wilson, the best candidate for President would most likely have to resemble which of the following cartoon characters?

(1) Daffy Duck
(2) Fred Flintstone
(3) Bugs Bunny
(4) Superman
(5) the Incredible Hulk

29. The author of the passage would be most likely to agree with which of these ideas?

(1) Executives should only be concerned with the overall picture.
(2) An understanding of a part helps in understanding the whole.
(3) Small ceremonies should not be duties of the President.
(4) If you take care of yourself, the details will take care of themselves.
(5) The Vice President should not perform any of the President's duties.

30. According to the passage, the duties of the President of the United States are which of the following?

(1) many and complex
(2) very easy
(3) being taken over by the Vice President
(4) routine
(5) inspiring

31. In 1995 the Food and Drug Administration declared nicotine a drug and proposed rules that would limit the promotion of tobacco products. The advertising industry, some of whose members represent tobacco companies, filed suit against the government. They argued that the rules violated their right to free speech. Based upon this principle, which of the following proposals would the advertisers most likely oppose?

(1) barring cigarette ads in publications that reach minors
(2) raising taxes on cigarettes
(3) banning cigarettes
(4) selling cigarettes only in bars
(5) banning the sale of cigarettes to minors

32. In 1954 the U.S. Supreme Court said in Brown v. Board of Education of Topeka, "We conclude that in the field of public education the doctrine of 'separate but equal' has no place. Separate educational facilities are inherently unequal."

This ruling most likely led to

(1) integration of private schools
(2) greater inequality in education
(3) more public schools
(4) better educational opportunities for all
(5) desegregation in public schools

Questions 33 through 36 refer to the following map.

Presidential Election, 1800

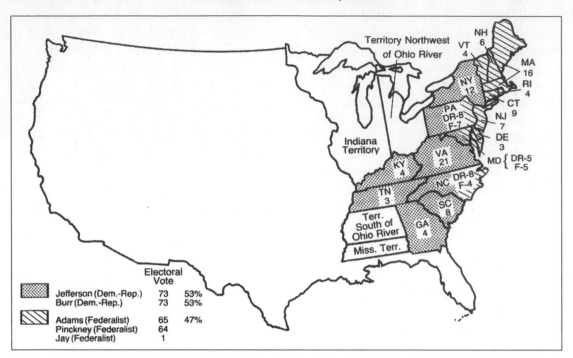

33. According to the map, how many states split their vote in the 1800 election?

    (1) three
    (2) four
    (3) five
    (4) six
    (5) seven

34. If the candidate receiving the most votes would become President, and the candidate with the second highest vote would become Vice President, why did the Federalist party cast one vote for Jay?

    (1) Only one state electoral voter disliked Pinckney.
    (2) It was a sympathy vote.
    (3) It was a strategy to guarantee Adams as President if the Federalist party had a majority.
    (4) The Maryland Federalists couldn't agree on which candidate was best.
    (5) Jay was not considered to be presidential material.

35. Which conclusion below does the information on the map best support?

    (1) A two-party system does not work.
    (2) Adams had little support in New England.
    (3) Electoral votes do not reflect the popular vote.
    (4) Electoral votes are more efficient than popular votes.
    (5) Indiana didn't have a vote because it wasn't a state.

36. Which of the following information is excluded from this map?

    (1) how many electoral votes each state had
    (2) how many votes each candidate received
    (3) who actually became President
    (4) which states participated in the election
    (5) who lost the election

Questions 37 and 38 refer to the following chart and passage.

Congressional Bills Vetoed, 1789–2000

President	Regular vetoes	Pocket vetoes	Total vetoes	Vetoes overridden	President	Regular vetoes	Pocket vetoes	Total vetoes	Vetoes overridden
Washington	2	—	2	—	Benjamin Harrison	19	25	44	1
John Adams	—	—	—	—	Cleveland	42	128	170	5
Jefferson	—	—	—	—	McKinley	6	36	42	—
Madison	5	2	7	—	Theodore Roosevelt	42	40	82	1
Monroe	1	—	1	—	Taft	30	9	39	1
John Q. Adams	—	—	—	—	Wilson	33	11	44	6
Jackson	5	7	12	—	Harding	5	1	6	
Van Buren	—	1	1	—	Coolidge	20	30	50	4
William Harrison	—	—	—	—	Hoover	21	16	37	3
Tyler	6	4	10	1	Franklin Roosevelt	372	263	635	9
Polk	2	1	3	—	Truman	180	70	250	12
Taylor	—	—	—	—	Eisenhower	73	108	181	2
Fillmore	—	—	—	—	Kennedy	12	9	21	—
Pierce	9	—	9	5	Lyndon Johnson	16	14	30	—
Buchanan	4	3	7	—	Nixon	26	17	43	7
Lincoln	2	4	6	—	Ford	48	18	66	12
Andrew Johnson	21	8	29	15	Carter	13	18	31	2
Grant	45	48	93	4	Reagan	39	39	78	9
Hayes	12	1	13	1	Bush	29	15	44	1
Garfield	—	—	—	—	Clinton	34	—	34	2
Arthur	4	8	12	1	**Total**	**1,482**	**1,064**	**2,546**	**106**
Cleveland	304	110	414	2					

One of the powers vested in the President is that of veto, as provided by Article I, Section 7 of the Constitution of the United States:

Every Bill which shall have passed the House of Representatives and the Senate, shall, before it become a Law, be presented to the President of the United States; If he approve he shall sign it, but if not he shall return it, with his Objections to that House in which it shall have originated, who shall enter the Objections at large on their Journal, and proceed to reconsider it. If after such Reconsideration two thirds of that House shall agree to pass the Bill, it shall be sent, together with the Objections, to the other House, by which it shall likewise be reconsidered, and if approved by two thirds of the House, it shall become a Law.... If any Bill shall not be returned by the President within ten Days (Sundays excepted) after it shall have been presented to him, the Same shall be a Law, in like Manner as if he had signed it, unless the Congress by their Adjournment prevent its Return, in which Case it shall not be a Law.

37. According to the passage, what is the most likely definition of the "pocket veto" mentioned in the chart?

(1) a veto that the President pockets and forgets about
(2) an unsigned bill that comes to the President just before a congressional adjournment
(3) a bill that is eventually passed
(4) a bill that is not returned to the sitting Congress for more than 10 days
(5) a bill that the President wants to think about for a long time

38. Which of the following is a conclusion that might be drawn from the chart?

(1) Vetoes were used more frequently in the twentieth century than in the nineteenth century.
(2) Only Presidents who served more than two terms used vetoes frequently.
(3) Lincoln used vetoes rarely because of the Civil War.
(4) Unpopular Presidents often have their vetoes overturned.
(5) Washington, Adams, and Jefferson probably didn't know how to use a pocket veto.

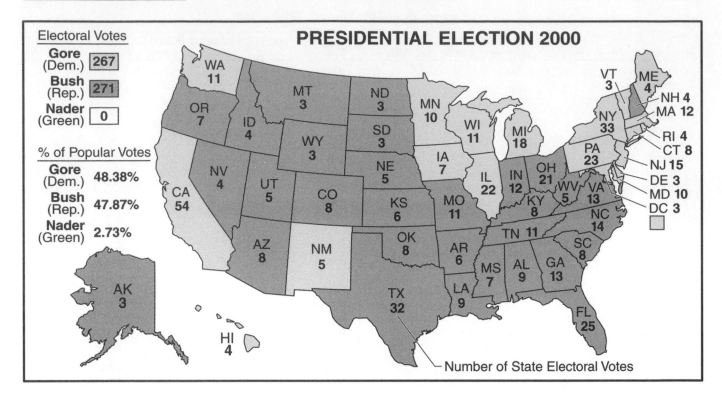

PRESIDENTIAL ELECTION 2000

Electoral Votes
Gore (Dem.) **267**
Bush (Rep.) **271**
Nader (Green) **0**

% of Popular Votes
Gore (Dem.) 48.38%
Bush (Rep.) 47.87%
Nader (Green) 2.73%

Number of State Electoral Votes

The 2000 Presidential Election will go down in history as a fascinating and contentious struggle, not so much between two candidates as among diverse institutions and political groups. The election was not decided on November 7, election day. Rather, it came to an end on December 13, when Vice President Gore telephoned his opponent George W. Bush, acknowledging defeat after a divided Supreme Court decision on the Florida recount. The 5 to 4 ruling, in the complex and contradictory decision announced at 10 P.M. on December 12, held that December 12 was the final deadline for naming electors and that, for all practical purposes, time had run out for any recount. Although Gore won the popular vote countrywide, when Florida electors cast their ballots for Bush, he won an electoral victory of 271 to Gore's 267.

39. What conclusion might be drawn from the information provided in the map?

(1) Bush carried the southern states.
(2) Gore was popular in the west.
(3) Bush won the popular vote in the most populous states.
(4) Gore won the popular vote in most states.
(5) Gore carried the Great Plains.

40. Which of the following can be inferred about the electoral college system, according to the passage and map?

(1) The electoral college expresses the will of the people.
(2) States may divide their electoral college votes among different candidates.
(3) The electoral college, not the majority of voters in the country, elects the President.
(4) Each state has the same number of electoral votes.
(5) It is impossible to win the popular vote and the electoral vote at the same time.

41. How did the Supreme Court affect the election?

(1) It ruled that Bush won.
(2) It stopped a recount.
(3) It required Florida to recount.
(4) It refused to hear Gore's side.
(5) It issued a ruling that confused both candidates.

Question 42 refers to the following passage.

Although acts of terrorism often occur in some countries, they are fairly rare in the United States. On April 19, 1995, a bomb exploded at a federal building in Oklahoma City, killing 168 people and injuring hundreds. The U.S. government responded with increased resolve to fight domestic terrorism. Federal officers from the FBI, the Justice Department, and the Bureau of Alcohol, Tobacco, and Firearms worked together to investigate the bombing. Local authorities also helped with the investigation.

42. Which of the following can be inferred from the passage about the U.S. government's response to the bombing in Oklahoma City?

   (1) stopping domestic terrorism is a top priority
   (2) law enforcement agencies work well together
   (3) local police are understaffed
   (4) terrorism is a problem for all countries
   (5) terrorism is as big a problem in the United States as it is in the rest of the world

---

Questions 43 and 44 refer to the following passage.

Health care costs in the United States are soaring. In 1998 U.S. citizens spent about $1.1 trillion dollars on healthcare, nearly thirty times what they spent in 1965.

Many people blame the rise in medical costs on expensive new technologies and treatments. Some say that costs are rising because the population is aging. Still others point to waste and fraud in the healthcare system.

In 1999 an estimated 42.5 million Americans were uninsured. One of the tragedies of high healthcare costs is that many people do not receive adequate medical care. As a result, some concerned citizens are calling for a national healthcare system that would cut costs and guarantee medical coverage for all Americans.

The federal government has provided healthcare for some of its citizens since the 1960s when Congress enacted two programs to provide healthcare coverage. Medicaid provides health coverage for the poor. Medicare provides health coverage for the elderly and the disabled.

Since the United States is already in debt, and healthcare programs are expensive, some Americans favor shrinking the deficit by cutting programs such as Medicare and Medicaid. However, politicians are afraid of angering a large voting population which would be affected by the cuts. In addition, some Americans think that cuts in these programs would increase the ranks of the uninsured.

Lawmakers will likely continue to grapple with this issue because they know that rising healthcare costs threaten the economic health of the country. They also know that the lack of affordable medical insurance threatens the physical health of Americans.

43. It can be inferred from the passage that some politicians are reluctant to cut Medicare benefits. Why?

   (1) Many lawmakers are elderly.
   (2) Senior citizens have political clout.
   (3) Waste in the healthcare system would increase.
   (4) It is a fairly small program.
   (5) It would increase the federal deficit.

44. Which of the following conclusions is supported by the passage?

   (1) Healthcare spending takes up too much of the gross national product.
   (2) State governments will have to take responsibility for healthcare.
   (3) People without health insurance can't afford care.
   (4) The rising cost of healthcare only affects the poor.
   (5) People may leave the country to obtain affordable care.

45. After World War II, "right-to-work" laws were passed by twenty states, barring labor unions from requiring membership as a condition of employment. Because labor unions have had a major role in American politics, what was most likely the effect of these laws?

They

(1) relieved some workers of unwanted political connections
(2) increased political activity on the part of the unions
(3) increased labor union strength in the other states
(4) influenced unions to affiliate with the Democratic party
(5) led to the end of labor unions in the twenty states

46. For raising operational monies, states rely primarily on sales taxes. Cities rely primarily on property taxes. When trying to attract new businesses from other states, what would a major city most likely try to offer the businesses?

(1) increased sales taxes
(2) decreased sales taxes
(3) a high property tax rate
(4) a low property tax rate
(5) a break on federal income taxes

47. Lawmakers sometimes fund projects in their home districts to curry favor with voters. They may also reward industries and special interest groups that support their campaign efforts. These practices are called pork-barrel politics and can come in the form of special projects funding attached to spending bills or, more recently, as relief from federal regulations. Which of the following best explains why it is so difficult to stop pork-barrel politics?

(1) All Americans benefit from the practice.
(2) Keeping voters and campaign contributors happy helps lawmakers get reelected.
(3) Lawmakers favor big business.
(4) Lawmakers are afraid of special interest groups.
(5) The practice is legal.

Question 48 refers to the following cartoon.

STEVE MCBRIDE Courtesy Independence Daily Reporter (Kan.)

48. Which of the following titles would best fit this cartoon?

(1) Politics—a Feeding Frenzy
(2) A Swine and a Swindle
(3) Hog Heaven
(4) Bringing Home the Bacon
(5) Living High Off the Hog

49. The 104th Congress, elected in 1994, promised major change in government. For the first time in many years, Republicans outnumbered Democrats in both houses of Congress even though the president at that time was a Democrat. What is the most likely result of having an activist Republican majority in Congress and a Democrat in the White House?

(1) more cooperation between Republicans and Democrats
(2) fewer presidential vetoes
(3) legislation that reflects a conservative agenda
(4) little change
(5) more Democrats joining the Republican party

UNIT 4 Economics

Directions: Choose the one best answer to each question.

Questions 1 and 2 refer to the following charts and information.

A country's balance of trade is the difference between the total value of a country's exports and the total value of its imports. If its total exports are more than its total imports, the country has a trade surplus. If its total imports are more than its total exports, it has a trade deficit.

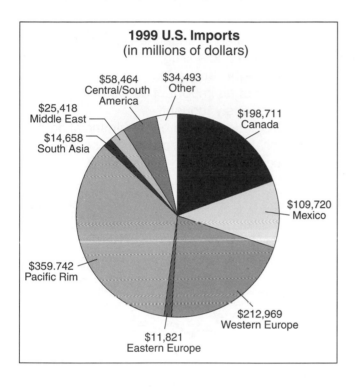

1999 U.S. Imports
(in millions of dollars)

$58,464 Central/South America
$34,493 Other
$25,418 Middle East
$14,658 South Asia
$198,711 Canada
$109,720 Mexico
$359,742 Pacific Rim
$212,969 Western Europe
$11,821 Eastern Europe

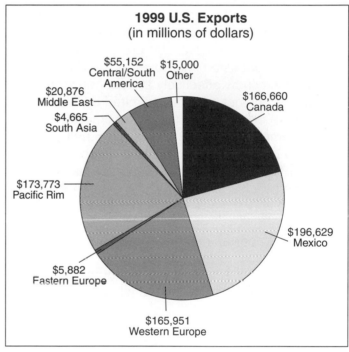

1999 U.S. Exports
(in millions of dollars)

$55,152 Central/South America
$15,000 Other
$20,876 Middle East
$4,665 South Asia
$166,660 Canada
$173,773 Pacific Rim
$196,629 Mexico
$5,882 Fastern Europe
$165,951 Western Europe

1. Based on its balance of trade for 1999, how could the United States be compared to a household?

   (1) has only one wage earner
   (2) shares its assets with a wide circle of friends and relatives
   (3) saves a significant portion of its income
   (4) spends more than it earns
   (5) is forced to spend much of its income on basic necessities like food and housing

2. Based on the information in the charts, which of the following would most likely have the greatest beneficial effect on the U.S. balance of trade?

   (1) U.S. factories using less oil from the Middle East
   (2) U.S. consumers buying fewer Pacific Rim cars and electronics
   (3) U.S. consumers buying fewer agricultural products from Africa
   (4) the U.S. increasing its volume of trade with other countries in the Americas
   (5) the U.S. decreasing its volume of trade with Eastern Europe

Questions 3 through 6 refer to the following passage.

Recent experience makes it clear that economists do not have all the answers to the many and varied economic issues and questions we confront both personally and as members of the larger socioeconomic system. Here are two examples. Although economists believe they now have the knowledge and tools to prevent massive economic depressions such as the one that occurred in the 1930s, much remains to be learned about how to moderate inflation while still holding down the rate of unemployment. And the issue of what the extent of the government's role in our economy should be remains unresolved.

There are several reasons why answers to the problems economists confront are not always found. Economic systems are complex and defy easy comprehension. Moreover, our ability to know exactly how effectively the economy and its components function is often limited by the difficulty of obtaining accurate and timely measurements of economic activity. Finally, a variety of unanticipated political and social events affects economic activity and makes accurate prediction of the results of economic decisions very difficult. Unlike in the physical sciences, carefully controlled experiments are difficult to undertake in economics.

3. The author suggests that economic prediction is difficult for which of these reasons?

(1) The experiments often go wrong.
(2) The instruments of economics are inaccurate.
(3) The quantity of people is often unknown.
(4) No real answers can be found.
(5) Depression gets to all of us.

4. Which of the following is another problem that illustrates the complexity of economic systems?

(1) having to balance a checkbook
(2) knowing how to moderate inflation while holding down unemployment
(3) determining the role of government in the economy
(4) having economists personally confront economic questions
(5) knowing how to balance the national budget without additional taxation

5. Which of the following is an opinion held by the author?

(1) Economists don't have all the answers.
(2) Economists can prevent economic depressions.
(3) Economists are members of a socioeconomic system.
(4) A massive depression occurred in the 1930s.
(5) Carefully controlled experiments can be conducted in the physical sciences.

6. The information in this passage supports which of these conclusions about the study of economics?

(1) It's limited to understanding patterns of buying and selling.
(2) It's highly accurate.
(3) It's not as important as we had previously thought.
(4) It's based on more than financial data.
(5) It's the most complex of the social sciences.

Questions 7 and 8 refer to the following cartoon.

Reprinted with special permission of King Features Syndicate, Inc.

7. What does the cartoon suggest about the federal deficit?

(1) It's a joking matter.
(2) It's a serious problem.
(3) It's something to ask your father about.
(4) It's under Mafia control.
(5) It's easily resolved.

8. The message of the cartoon is based on a reference to which of the following?

(1) careful budgeting
(2) analytical questioning
(3) reckless gambling
(4) the greater good
(5) rational expenditure

Questions 9 through 12 refer to the following definitions.

sole proprietorship—a business owned and operated by one person who receives all profits and is responsible for all debts

partnership—a business owned by two or more people who share the profits and responsibility for any debts

corporation—a business that is a legal entity, distinct from its owners, which acts as one body. Owners purchase shares of stock in the corporation. Share owners are called stockholders and are not legally liable for the business's debts.

9. After fifteen years of being partners with Mr. Allen in a pottery business, Mrs. Peters has decided to open her own business. What should she do to dissolve the partnership?

    (1) refuse to pay any of the pottery business's debts
    (2) put a notice in the paper declaring she is no longer responsible for any of Mr. Allen's debts
    (3) sell Mr. Allen her part of the business.
    (4) simply establish sole proprietorship of her own pottery business
    (5) quit working with Mr. Allen

10. Which of the following is one major problem for people starting their own businesses?

    (1) having to set their own hours
    (2) making all the profit
    (3) finding a market for their businesses
    (4) getting large loans from banks
    (5) deciding which accounting method to use

11. Which of the following would most likely happen if one shareholder in a corporation died?

    (1) The corporation would be dissolved.
    (2) The shares would automatically be divided among the other stockholders.
    (3) The ownership of the shares would be transferred to any heirs, who could either keep or sell them.
    (4) The other stockholders would be liable for the shareholder's debts.
    (5) The corporation could not function until the shares were sold to someone else.

12. Which of the following statements is best supported by the definitions?

    (1) The establishment and management of a corporation is more complex than that of a partnership.
    (2) A partnership is a more profitable type of business organization than a sole proprietorship.
    (3) The transfer of stock within a corporation is a time-consuming process
    (4) A stockholder is never at any financial risk.
    (5) A business owned by a sole proprietor can be sold more easily than one owned in partnership.

Question 13 refers to the following graph.

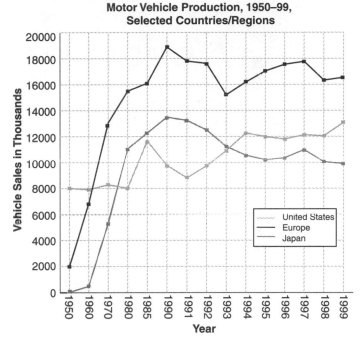

Motor Vehicle Production, 1950–99, Selected Countries/Regions

13. If vehicle sales are a sign of economic health, what might be concluded from the graph?

    (1) Japan saw a major depression in the 1980s.
    (2) The United States and Europe experienced economic declines in the late 1990s.
    (3) Europe is healthier economically than the United States.
    (4) Both Europe and Japan may have suffered an economic decline in the early 1990s.
    (5) The United States produced more cars per capita than Europe.

Two important economic principles are the laws of supply and demand. The law of supply is that as the price of a product or service increases, the supplier usually wants to provide more to the consumer. The law of demand is that as prices decrease, the consumer usually will want to buy more.

14. Which of the following is an example of the law of demand?

    (1) As gasoline prices rise, people don't drive any less.
    (2) A local supermarket offers more kinds of bread.
    (3) Automobile dealers lower prices and offer cash rebates in order to increase sales.
    (4) A two-pack-a-day smoker continues the habit even though the price of cigarettes goes up.
    (5) Sales of personal computers decline as they become more widely used.

15. From the standpoint of the laws of supply and demand, which of the following steps could a government take to decrease teenage unemployment?

    (1) make the minimum wage lower for teenagers than for other workers
    (2) set up training programs for unemployed youths
    (3) establish numerical quotas that businesses must adhere to
    (4) develop education curricula based on the needs of businesses and other employers
    (5) lower the age at which students can leave school, so that more teenagers can become part of the workforce

16. Falling real-estate prices encourage more people to buy homes. But as prices fall, fewer and fewer homeowners want to put their homes up for sale. Eventually, there is a shortage of houses for sale, and home prices rise again. What does this show about the laws of supply and demand?

    (1) They interact to bring prices to a balance point.
    (2) The law of supply is stronger.
    (3) The law of demand is stronger.
    (4) The working of the laws are affected by the particular industry and situation.
    (5) Prices and supplies of goods are determined both by the laws of supply and demand and by consumer behavior.

17. A notecard manufacturer notices that retail outlets continue to order the same amount after the wholesale price is raised from $0.60 to $0.75. What action will the manufacturer most likely take?

    (1) lower prices again to sell even more cards
    (2) increase the wholesale price again
    (3) continue to produce the same number of cards to sell at $0.75 each
    (4) manufacture fewer cards
    (5) find more outlets and make more cards

The laws of supply and demand apply to some products more than others. When consumption is not affected much by rising or falling prices, we say that demand is inelastic. Usually, demand for products that people often consume, such as milk, is relatively inelastic. Demand for other products, such as air travel, is elastic. As airfares go on sale, as during a fare war, demand increases.

18. For which one of the following items is demand relatively inelastic?

    (1) chicken and beef
    (2) cheese and yogurt
    (3) peaches and cherries
    (4) salt and pepper
    (5) cakes and other deserts

Questions 19 through 22 refer to the following graph and passage.

**Gasoline Retail Prices,
Selected Countries, 1990–1999**
(taxes and fees included)

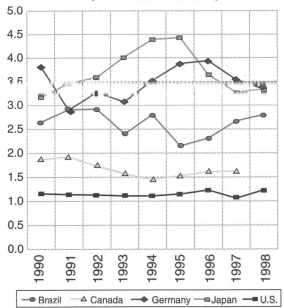

20. If average vehicle consumption in the United States has decreased over the last decade, what probably explains the increase in petroleum consumption?

    (1) an increase in products and services that use petroleum and its products
    (2) a decrease in fees and taxes on gas
    (3) an increase in oil prices
    (4) greater environmental consciousness among consumers
    (5) an increase in mass transit use

21. Which of the following is a conclusion that can be drawn from the evidence in the passage and the graph?

    (1) There is a direct correspondence between low gasoline prices and high petroleum consumption.
    (2) Petroleum is used to produce fuels.
    (3) High petroleum production encourages low gasoline prices.
    (4) The United States is the greatest producer of petroleum.
    (5) China and Russia probably have low gasoline prices.

22. Which country saw the steepest decline in gasoline prices?

    (1) the United States
    (2) Brazil
    (3) Canada
    (4) Japan
    (5) Germany

Gasoline prices and the automotive industry are tightly intertwined economically, insofar as motor vehicles are the largest users of gasoline world-wide. The early 1970s through the 1980s, gasoline crises encouraged motorists, especially U.S. motorists with their large gas-guzzlers, to purchase small, fuel-efficient cars. However, during the 1990s, production of petroleum (from which gasoline is derived) rose substantially from 64.4 million barrels per day to 72.8 million barrels per day (from 1989-1998). With increasing crude oil availability, the United States enjoyed relatively low gasoline prices. It should come as no surprise that of world petroleum consumers, the United States ranks first, with a consumption rate of 18.9 million barrels per day. Japan is a distant second, with 5.5 million barrels per day. China, Germany and Russia follow.

19. If petroleum is available world-wide at approximately the same price, which of the following best explains why prices differ?

    (1) taxes and fees levied
    (2) transportation
    (3) supply and demand
    (4) vehicle consumption
    (5) altitude

At the same time production does remain important and urgent for its effect on economic security. When men are unemployed, society does not miss the goods they do not produce. The loss here is marginal. But the men who are without work do miss the income they no longer earn. Here the effect is not marginal. It involves all or a large share of the men's earnings and hence all or a large share of what they are able to buy. And, we note, high and stable production is the broad foundation of the economic security of virtually every other group—of farmers, white-collar workers, and both large businessmen and small. The depression also remains the major uncovered risk of the modern large corporation. It is for reasons of economic security that we must produce at capacity.

23. Which of the following proverbs best summarizes the author's assumption about goods that are not produced?

    (1) Absence makes the heart grow fonder.
    (2) Out of sight, out of mind.
    (3) You don't miss your water 'til your well runs dry.
    (4) Better late than never.
    (5) Don't cut off your nose to spite your face.

24. The passage assumes that an economy is based primarily on which of the following?

    (1) agriculture
    (2) manufacturing
    (3) services (retail, etc.)
    (4) high-tech industries
    (5) international trade

25. According to the passage, which of the following would be only marginally affected by low levels of production?

    (1) unemployment
    (2) spending
    (3) buying power
    (4) personal income
    (5) demand for certain goods

26. Which of the following is potentially an extreme result of low production?

    (1) depression
    (2) overspending
    (3) socialism
    (4) communism
    (5) low unemployment

27. Which of the following conclusions is best supported by the passage?

    (1) Too many people are unemployed.
    (2) The product itself is less important than the production of it.
    (3) Our society is too concerned with material goods.
    (4) The policies of modern corporations are leading to another depression.
    (5) Capacity of production will solve all economic problems.

Question 28 refers to the following table.

U.S. Computer Ownership by Characteristic, 1998

Characteristic Ethnicity	Total U.S.	Characteristic Age	Total U.S.
White non-Hispanic	46.6%	Under 25 years	32.3%
Black non-Hispanic	23.2%	25–34 years	46.0%
AIEA* non-Hispanic	34.3%	35–44 years	54.9%
API** non-Hispanic	55.0%	45–54 years	54.7%
Hispanic	25.5%	55+ years	25.8%

Characteristic—Income	Total U.S.
Under $5,000	15.9%
$ 5,000–$9,999	12.3%
$10,000–$14,999	15.9%
$15,000–$19,999	21.2%
$20,000–$24,999	25.7%
$25,000–$34,999	35.8%
$35,000–$49,999	50.2%
$50,000–$74,999	66.3%
$75,000+	79.9%

*American Indian, Eskimo, Aleut
**Asian, Pacific Islander

28. What characteristic most affects computer ownership in the U.S.?

    (1) age
    (2) education
    (3) ethnicity
    (4) income
    (5) location

Question 29 refers to the following cartoon.

©Donrey Media Group for "Small Business Cartoon" by David Cox (Hardin). Reprinted by permission of NW Arkansas Morning News.

29. The cartoon suggests which of the following ideas?

(1) Current economic conditions favor small businesses.
(2) The construction industry is subject to unfair taxes.
(3) Taxes on all businesses are too high.
(4) High taxes are making it difficult for small businesses to succeed.
(5) Small business owners try to avoid paying taxes.

Question 30 refers to the following passage.

Unlike private pension plans, in which contributions are saved until the individual's retirement, Social Security is financed through taxes on the earnings of current workers. Both the employee and the employer contribute percentage amounts. Employers withhold the employee's contributions and remit those and their own contributions to the Internal Revenue Service. All Social Security taxes are transferred to the Social Security Trust Funds and are either saved for future benefits or paid out to current beneficiaries.

30. Which of the following is most like the funding mechanism of Social Security?

(1) an individual savings account
(2) a lottery ticket
(3) a stock investment
(4) a raffle drawing
(5) a medical insurance plan

Questions 31 and 32 refer to the following cartoon.

©1993 by Chester Commodore, in the Chicago Defender. Reprinted with permission.

31. Which of the following can be inferred from the cartoon?

(1) Everyone entering the building will get a job.
(2) Most workers prefer part-time jobs.
(3) The people leaving the building no longer want long-term jobs.
(4) It is better to work for a large corporation than a small one.
(5) Many long-term workers are losing their jobs.

32. What conclusion can be drawn from the cartoon?

(1) Large corporations no longer offer long-term job security.
(2) Not all workers want long-term jobs.
(3) Part-time jobs are easy to find.
(4) Most workers want to work for big corporations.
(5) Small corporations are good places to look for long-term jobs.

Questions 33 through 35 are based on the following information.

Annual Percent Change in Consumer Price Indexes: 1988–1999

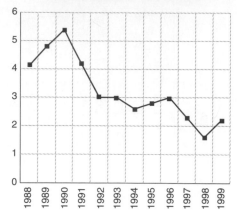

The Consumer Price Index (CPI) measures the average change in prices over time for a fixed group of goods and services used by the typical urban wage-earner.

33. According to the passage, what effect might an increase in the price of oil have on the economy?

    (1) increase employment
    (2) raise the CPI
    (3) lower the CPI
    (4) spur spending
    (5) no effect

34. The drop in the CPI from 1990 to 1998 was most likely due to which of the following?

    (1) the congressional elections
    (2) high employment in Asian and European countries
    (3) decreasing gasoline prices
    (4) low unemployment
    (5) increasing internet use

35. After years of neglect, transportation systems across the country were upgraded in the early 1990s, improving service but also raising fares. How might these improvements affect the CPI?

    (1) Increasing transportation costs might increase the CPI.
    (2) Increasing transportation costs might lower the CPI.
    (3) Improved transportation systems might lower the CPI.
    (4) Increased employment might lower the CPI.
    (5) There would be no effect.

Question 36 refers to the following passage.

In 1998, the Socialist Republic of Vietnam exported $9.4 billion in products (primarily crude oil, marine products, rice, coffee, rubber, etc.) and imported $11.4 billion in products (primarily machinery and equipment, petroleum products, fertilizer, steel products, etc.). For years, the United States had imposed a trade embargo on its former enemy. In 1994, the U.S. lifted that embargo.

36. How might the lifting of the embargo improve the Vietnamese economy?

    (1) More U.S. products might be sold to Vietnam.
    (2) Fewer Vietnamese products might be sold to Korea.
    (3) More Vietnamese products might be purchased by the U.S.
    (4) More banks might make loans to Vietnam.
    (5) Factories in Vietnam might purchase U.S. machines.

Questions 37 through 40 refer to the following graphs.

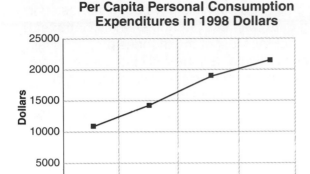

Per Capita Personal Consumption Expenditures in 1998 Dollars

Source: U.S. Dept. of Commerce

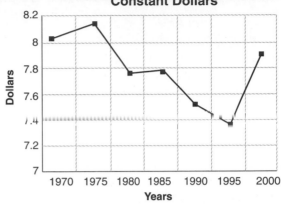

Average Hourly Earnings in 1982 Constant Dollars

Source: U.S. Dept. of Labor

37. Which of the following conclusions can be drawn from the information in the graphs?

People will be

(1) very budget-conscious
(2) attentive to the inflation rate
(3) living beyond their means
(4) spending money no matter what their wages are
(5) spending more money as they get older

38. The decrease in average hourly earnings from 1975 to 1995 is most likely a reflection of which of the following?

(1) a decrease in the minimum wage
(2) an increase in the minimum wage
(3) a depression
(4) a change in the level of productivity
(5) increased taxation

39. If the wage trend shown in the graphs continues, what can you conclude about the likely experience of the next generation?

The next generation will

(1) have a lower standard of living than we do now
(2) live better than we do now
(3) live about the same way as we do now
(4) spend more money than we do now
(5) live in poverty

40. The information in the graphs best supports which of the following statements?

(1) Real earning has seen a net decrease.
(2) A decrease in the hourly wage rate leads to a corresponding decrease in spending.
(3) Over the past 15 years hourly wages have increased at a faster rate than inflation.
(4) The economy has been very unstable over the past 15 years.
(5) Spending will always outpace earning.

Questions 41 and 42 refer to the following passage.

Production of any product or service requires three basic ingredients. The first of these, labor, is the human effort involved. The second ingredient is capital. Capital, or money, also includes all the other products necessary to produce something. The third ingredient includes the supplies or resources provided by nature.

41. Which of the following is important capital for the production of furniture?

(1) carpenters
(2) tools
(3) trees
(4) sawmill operators
(5) cotton

42. Which of the following businesses would be most likely to spend the largest percentage of money on natural resources for its production of goods or services?

    (1) an oil company
    (2) a retail liquor store
    (3) a computer software company
    (4) a housekeeping service
    (5) an athletic shoe manufacturer

Questions 43 and 44 refer to the following cartoon.

"Yes, this is the dotty old lady of the house, but no I don't want to buy any of your penny stocks."

By C. Barsotti, USA TODAY. Copyright 1989, USA TODAY. Reprinted by permission.

43. Which opinion is the cartoonist expressing?

    (1) Some investment firms try to take advantage of senior citizens.
    (2) Older people are not interested in investments.
    (3) Not even cheap stocks justify rudeness.
    (4) Penny stocks are not a wise investment.
    (5) Investment transactions should never be conducted over the telephone.

44. Of the following, which would most likely describe the caroonist?

    (1) an advocate of penny stocks
    (2) an opponent of penny stocks
    (3) a financial expert
    (4) an advocate of consumer protection laws
    (5) an opponent of consumer protection laws

Question 45 refers to the following passage.

The business cycle characterizes most modern economies. Economists have been interested in trying to explain this phenomenon since the early 19th century. Most of the theories proposed fall into one of two categories: (1) Economies have basic flaws which lead to cycles. These cycles can only be controlled through outside intervention; and (2) Outside interference leads to swings between high and low employment that are the cause of the business cycles. Still, many economists are uncertain about the true cause of business cycles and about the cure. After World War II, the U.S. government adjusted tax policy and government spending and controlled the nation's money supply in order to limit large fluctuations in the economy. However, by the 1990s the U.S. economy was still subject to the boom and bust cycle.

45. A proponent of the first theory of business cycles would probably support which of the following?

    (1) the establishment of a flat tax rate for all Americans
    (2) the further deregulation of the banking industry
    (3) eliminating subsidies and supports for farmers
    (4) stricter control of the money supply by the Federal Reserve
    (5) reducing or eliminating welfare programs

Directions: Choose the one best answer to each question.

Questions 1 through 3 refer to the following passage.

For several weeks early every spring, thousands of sandhill cranes land on the banks of the Platte River near Kearney, Nebraska. Here they feed and rest for their long northward migration. But this section of the Platte, once almost a mile wide, has been reduced to only several hundred feet by upstream dams which regulate the early spring floods. The cranes' natural rest stop may be further threatened by the building of a new dam that would divert water from the Platte for the use of Denver and possibly other cities. This project has resulted in a dispute between the water planners and environmentalists.

1. Which of the following statements is suggested by the passage?

   (1) The sandhill crane population is in danger of extinction.
   (2) Nebraska no longer receives enough rainfall.
   (3) Flooding is still a problem for Denver and other cities.
   (4) Denver does not have an adequate water supply.
   (5) The Platte River is more than sufficient for the needs of both humans and birds.

2. If other areas follow the example of diverting water from already depleted rivers, the result will most likely be which of the following?

   (1) the further growth of cities in water-poor areas
   (2) a mass relocation of animal sanctuaries
   (3) a serious environmental problem
   (4) a revitalization of river systems
   (5) a whole new network of rivers

3. Which of the following statements is most likely to be an argument presented in favor of the dam project?

   (1) Human use of resources is more important than preservation of bird habitat.
   (2) The birds can easily find somewhere else to rest.
   (3) About half the water will be needed for watering lawns.
   (4) Annual flooding will still take place on the Platte River.
   (5) The cranes will be allowed to use the dam's reservoir as a watering hole.

Question 4 refers to the following graph and passage.

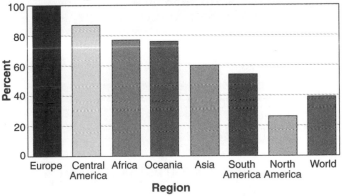

Percentage of Forest Under Threat of Destruction

One of the major threats to forests is acid rain, created when sulfur dioxide and nitrogen dioxides combine with moisture in the air. Oil and coal combustion along with automobile emissions are the cause of most acid rain.

4. Which of the following actions has most likely been enacted in response to the situation described above?

   (1) lowering of emission standards in the United States
   (2) strict emission controls in Europe
   (3) logging restrictions in Asia
   (4) restrictions on architectural use of wood in North America
   (5) increased use of bamboo in Oceania

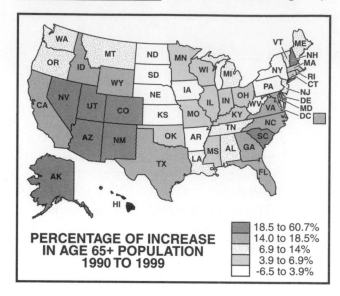

PERCENTAGE OF INCREASE
IN AGE 65+ POPULATION
1990 TO 1999

18.5 to 60.7%
14.0 to 18.5%
6.9 to 14%
3.9 to 6.9%
-6.5 to 3.9%

5. Which of the following is a conclusion that can be drawn from the map?

   (1) Elderly people usually stay in their original geographical location.
   (2) Southern and western states have seen a rise in aging population.
   (3) The Midwest has seen the greatest increase in aging population.
   (4) Many people move to New York to retire.
   (5) Northern states have a very high standard of living.

6. Which of the following states has seen the most dramatic rise in 65+ population?

   (1) Oklahoma
   (2) Idaho
   (3) Alaska
   (4) Louisiana
   (5) Florida

7. According to evidence provided in the map, which of the following public facilities might have increased in number in Nevada?

   (1) high schools
   (2) colleges
   (3) casinos
   (4) elder care centers
   (5) libraries

Questions 8 and 9 refer to the following passage.

Hurricanes are large rotating tropical storms. Forming over oceans, they have winds of up to 150 miles per hour and torrential rains that can produce almost instant flooding.

8. People living in hurricane-prone areas would be most likely to prefer which of the following architectural features?

   (1) dirt floor cellars
   (2) high-rise apartment buildings
   (3) glass-enclosed patios
   (4) ranch style buildings
   (5) New England style gable roofs

9. Based on the passage, where are hurricanes most likely to occur?

   Where

   (1) the air is warm and moist
   (2) there are cool air masses
   (3) a large land mass is next to water
   (4) temperatures drop sharply
   (5) humidity is consistently low

10. In 1957 France, Belgium, Luxembourg, West Germany, Italy, and the Netherlands formed the European Economic Community, also known as the Common Market. This move improved their economies by removing the tariffs (taxes) on mutually imported or exported goods. When Denmark and Great Britain joined the group, why did the Common Market continue to make sense?

    Because

    (1) all Western European nations are in financial trouble
    (2) shipping distances between the nations are quite small
    (3) world peace depends on the cooperation of dissimilar cultures
    (4) each nation grows completely different crops
    (5) all these nations have adjoining borders

Questions 11 and 12 refer to the following map.

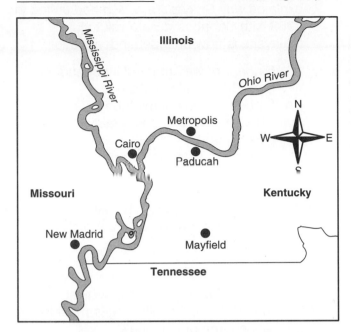

11. Which of the following statements is contrary to information found on the map?

    (1) The Mississippi River forms a natural boundary between Illinois and Missouri.
    (2) The Ohio River forms a natural boundary between Kentucky and Illinois.
    (3) Three states meet at the junction of two rivers.
    (4) The natural boundary between Missouri and Kentucky is the Ohio River.
    (5) It is possible to travel on the Ohio River to the Mississippi River.

12. At which of the following cities would a shipping company be most likely to set up a main office?

    (1) Paducah
    (2) Metropolis
    (3) Mayfield
    (4) Cairo
    (5) New Madrid

Questions 13 through 15 refer to the following passage.

Latitude and longitude are imaginary lines that form a grid pattern around the earth. Latitudes, or parallels, run east and west at equal distances from each other, never meeting. Latitudes are measured in degrees (°) northward from the Equator (0°) to the North Pole (90°N) and southward to the South Pole (90°S). Longitudes, or meridians, run north and south meeting at the poles. These lines are measured eastward for 180° from the Prime Meridian in Greenwich, England, and westward for 180°.

13. From the passage, which of the following can be assumed for Greenwich, England?

    It is located at

    (1) 0° latitude
    (2) 180° E longitude
    (3) 90° W longitude
    (4) 0° longitude
    (5) the Equator

14. For which of the following would knowledge of longitude and latitude be most important?

    (1) river transportation
    (2) city driving
    (3) ocean navigation
    (4) rural driving
    (5) cross-country hiking

15. Which of the following accurately states a difference between latitude and longitude?

    (1) Only lines of latitude are imaginary lines.
    (2) Only lines of latitude are measured in degrees beginning with 0.
    (3) Only lines of longitude are closer to one another at some points than at others.
    (4) Only lines of longitude differ from one another in length.
    (5) Only lines of longitude are measured north and south to the poles.

Questions 16 through 19 refer to the following maps.

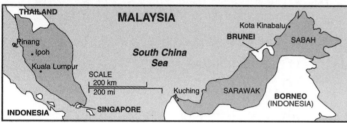

16. Which of the following is a country outside of Malaysia?

   (1) Kuala Lumpur
   (2) Ipoh
   (3) Brunei
   (4) Kuching
   (5) Kota Kinabalu

17. People living in East Malaysia probably find trade easiest with which of these countries?

   (1) Thailand
   (2) Australia
   (3) China
   (4) Indonesia
   (5) Vietnam

18. Which of the following statements best explains why Singapore, which had united in 1963 with Sabah and Sarawak to join Malaysia, is now an independent nation?

   (1) Singapore was granted independence from British rule in 1957.
   (2) Singapore was dominated by a Chinese, rather than a Malay, government.
   (3) The island was too far from the Malay Peninsula.
   (4) The islanders felt isolated.
   (5) Officials in Singapore believed that Sabah and Sarawak were too close to the island.

19. Considering Malaysia's geographical location, which of the following is most likely a recent source of revenue?

   (1) wool and mohair
   (2) off-shore oil
   (3) low-sulphur coal
   (4) beef cattle
   (5) wheat and corn

Question 20 refers to the following information.

   The weather of a region is the state of its atmosphere at a given time regarding characteristics like temperature and humidity. Its climate is the average of these characteristics over an extended period of time.

20. Which of the following is a description of climate?

   (1) Florida is experiencing an unusually cold winter.
   (2) Florida's winters are somewhat cooler than its summers.
   (3) In 1991 Florida was hit by a devastating hurricane.
   (4) Florida received a record-high amount of precipitation this year.
   (5) Florida is a major producer of oranges and grapefruit.

Questions 21 through 23 refer to the following map and passage.

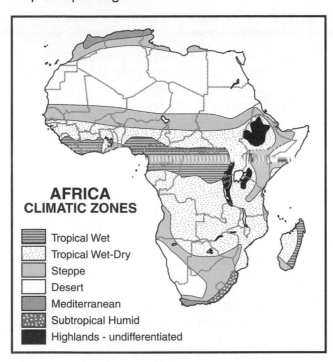

**AFRICA
CLIMATIC ZONES**

- Tropical Wet
- Tropical Wet-Dry
- Steppe
- Desert
- Mediterranean
- Subtropical Humid
- Highlands - undifferentiated

The climate of Africa falls into six zones (plus the undifferentiated highlands). Small strips of temperate, Mediterranean areas dot the upper and lower extremities. Along the coast of South Africa lies a subtropical humid zone similar to the Southeastern United States. Along the west coast in Southern Africa and in much of the northern areas lie the desert areas, where temperatures as high as 136 degrees Fahrenheit have been recorded. Along the desert border run very dry tropical steppes. These are in turn bordered by the savanna, which is wetter but still prone to dry spells. The interior tropical wet climate is hot and subject to even, steady rainfall.

21. Which of the following climate zones borders Africa's largest desert zone?

    (1) tropical wet
    (2) Mediterranean
    (3) steppes
    (4) desert
    (5) highlands

22. What zone has probably attracted the lowest population density?

    (1) Mediterranean
    (2) subtropical
    (3) tropical wet-dry
    (4) desert
    (5) coastal steppe

23. Which of the following best describes the climate of Africa's northern most tip?

    (1) temperate
    (2) steppe
    (3) highlands
    (4) subtropical
    (5) desert

Question 24 refers to the following map.

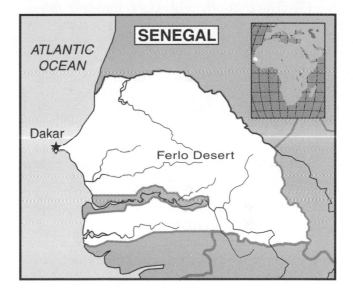

24. Given Senegal's location and geographical features, which of the following is a likely export?

    (1) fish
    (2) lumber
    (3) hydroelectric power
    (4) roses
    (5) wine

Questions 25 through 27 refer to the following passage.

Demography is the study of population, especially measurable aspects such as size, growth, geographic distribution, and composition in terms of gender and age. Demographers look at density of population, measured as the number of people living in a square mile of land. They look at changes in population size and growth resulting from changes in birth rates and death rates. These are just two examples of demography.

25. Which of the following best exemplifies a demographic explanation of a decline in a city's crime rate?

    (1) More police officers have been hired to patrol the streets.
    (2) Stricter laws have led to more arrests and more convictions.
    (3) The proportion of young males, a group disproportionately involved in crime, has fallen.
    (4) Drugs are a major factor in many crimes, and an antidrug campaign has decreased their availability.
    (5) Stricter gun control laws have reduced the number of guns.

26. Which of the following lies outside the scope of demography?

    (1) Highway planners want to know where people live and work.
    (2) A toy manufacturer needs to know how many children there are in an area where it wants to advertise.
    (3) Members of Congress who plan to overhaul Medicare want to know how many retirees there are now and will be in the future.
    (4) Disaster consultants in an area prone to earthquakes want to know if people living there are aware of precautions.
    (5) City planners want to estimate the number of children who will be born in the next decade, to decide whether new schools are needed.

27. Which of the following examples falls into a different study area than demography?

    (1) In 1966 New Zealand had a population density of 23 people per square mile.
    (2) In 1980 there were as many people over the age of 30 in the United States as there were under 30.
    (3) Between 1940 and 1950, the population of South Dakota rose by only 1.5%.
    (4) Indiana has a land area of 35,932 square miles.
    (5) New York City, with over 7,322,000 inhabitants, is one of the larger metropolitan nuclei in the United States.

Questions 28 and 29 refer to the following passage.

Scientists have found evidence that Earth is warming up because of the greenhouse effect. Since 1982, the temperature of the world's oceans has risen 0.2° Fahrenheit each year. The greenhouse effect occurs because gases, such as carbon dioxide, in Earth's atmosphere trap heat that Earth's surface gives off when hit by solar energy. The amount of carbon dioxide in the atmosphere has been increasing, mainly as a result of our use of fossil fuels.

28. Which of the following statements is supported by the passage?

    (1) Global warming has become the most serious environmental threat.
    (2) The greenhouse effect is solely the result of human activities.
    (3) Scientists need to find a way to eliminate the greenhouse effect.
    (4) Human activities have affected the environment in unforseen ways.
    (5) Global warming has seriously affected oceans and other large bodies of water.

29. If the gases that result from the use of fossil fuels are partially responsible for this problem, which of the choices below represents our best course of action?

    (1) start using oil instead of coal and gas
    (2) find alternate sources of energy
    (3) find a way to cool the oceans
    (4) find a way to contain the gases
    (5) prepare for warmer winters

Question 30 refers to the following map.

North America in 1783

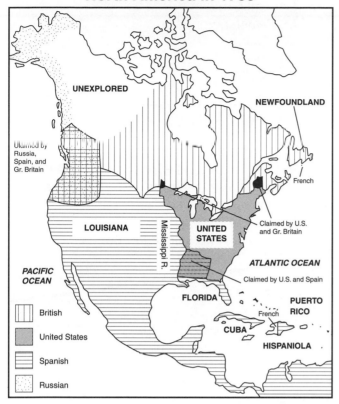

30. Which of the following is best explained by the information on this map?

    (1) the location of the Mexico-United States border
    (2) the purchase of the Louisiana Territory from France by the United States
    (3) the importance of the Mississippi River to the United States economy
    (4) the prevalence of Spanish place names in California
    (5) the definition of the Canada-United States border

Questions 31 through 33 refer to the following map and passage.

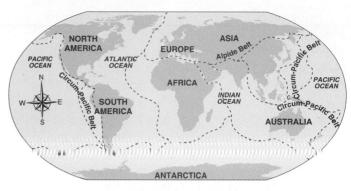

Although geological faults can be found worldwide, almost all of the major earthquakes occur in the Circum-Pacific and the Alpide belts. The San Andreas fault, along the west coast of the United States, is found in the Circum-Pacific zone. The Alpide belt denotes where Eurasia collided with the continent of Africa and the land mass that is now India.

31. Which of the following countries might be relatively unaffected by earthquakes?

    (1) Norway
    (2) Turkey
    (3) United States
    (4) Australia
    (5) Peru

32. According to the map, with which of the following are earthquakes most frequently associated?

    (1) rivers
    (2) lakes
    (3) oceans
    (4) mountains
    (5) valleys

33. Which of the following major world cities would most likely be affected by earthquakes?

    (1) New York, New York
    (2) Chicago, Illinois
    (3) Sidney, Australia
    (4) Johannesburg, South Africa
    (5) Acapulco, Mexico

Questions 34 through 37 refer to the following passage.

The state of Oregon has over 97,000 square miles of land. It is surrounded by the Pacific Ocean and the states of Washington, Idaho, Nevada, and California. The western third of Oregon is dramatically divided from the rest of the state by the Cascade Mountain Range. To the west of the Cascades, the land is drenched in rain for most of the year and is lush with vegetation. To the east of the Cascades, dust storms parch the land to the extent that many of the lakes listed on maps are referred to as dry. Much of Oregon is forested, even to the east where the woodlands are scattered and less dense. But due to the ever-increasing need for lumber, even the forests in the mountains and to the west are being cut too quickly for new growth to replace the old.

34. Which of the following statements best explains why the Bureau of Land Management might support the recycling of paper?

(1) The steady rainfalls in western Oregon occur through most of the year.
(2) Large-scale forest fires are frequent.
(3) Tree-planting teams have been working on reforestation for at least twenty years.
(4) Oregon was one of the first states to pass a bottle recycling bill.
(5) There are not enough lumber mills in Oregon.

35. Which of the following slogans is supported by information in the passage?

(1) Only You Can Prevent Forest Fires
(2) It's More Than a Tree; It's a Home
(3) Oregonians Don't Tan; They Rust
(4) Go West, Young Man
(5) Keep Our Cities Clean

36. Why is eastern Oregon drier than the western section?

(1) There is more land to the east.
(2) Many of the lakes have long since dried up.
(3) Frequent storms carry moisture into Washington.
(4) The Cascades block the wet ocean winds.
(5) The scattered forests don't retain much moisture.

37. Crops grown in eastern Oregon are most likely similar to those grown in

(1) California
(2) Washington
(3) Ohio
(4) Iowa
(5) Idaho

Questions 38 and 39 refer to the following graph and information.

Arable land is ground which can be cultivated. Land must be arable in order for crops to be planted and food grown on it.

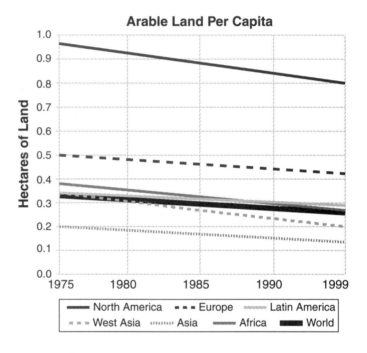

38. Which regions are most similar in the amount of land per capita?

(1) North America and Latin America
(2) North America and Europe
(3) Africa and Latin America
(4) Latin America and West Asia
(5) North America and Asia

39. What general trend does the graph show for global arable land?

(1) a rise in total arable land
(2) a slow decline in total arable land
(3) a slow decline in arable land per person
(4) a rise in arable land in the U.S.
(5) a precipitous rise in agricultural population

Questions 40 through 44 refer to the following table.

Urbanization in Selected Countries

Country	Urban population				Population in cities of 1 million +			Population in largest city		Average annual rate of increase in population (as of 2000)
	in millions		% of total		% of total population			% of urban population		% increase annualy
	1980	1998	1980	1998	1980	1995	2015	1980	1995	
Canada	18.6	23.3	76	77	29	36	35	16	19	0.4
China	191.3	003.7	20	31	0	11	14	0	4	0.0
Ethiopia	4.0	10.2	11	17	3	4	7	30	28	2.8
Jordan	1.3	3.3	60	73	29	28	35	49	39	2.4
Mexico	44.8	70.9	66	74	27	28	26	31	25	1.8
Pakistan	23.2	47.3	28	36	11	19	25	22	23	2.3
Singapore	2.3	3.2	100	100	100	100	86	100	100	0.86
Thailand	7.9	12.8	17	21	10	11	15	59	55	0.9
United States	167.5	207.5	74	77	36	39	39	9	8	0.55
Venezuela	12.0	20.1	79	86	16	27	28	21	16	1.6

40. Which country saw the greatest numerical rise in urban population from 1980 to 1998?

    (1) China
    (2) United States
    (3) Mexico
    (4) Pakistan
    (5) Singapore

41. Which of these countries had the greatest proportion of its urban population in its largest city in 1995?

    (1) Jordan
    (2) China
    (3) Thailand
    (4) United States
    (5) Venezuela

42. Based on information in the table, which of the following cities, each the largest in its country, is <u>most likely</u> to need to plan carefully for a growing population?

    (1) Addis Ababa, Ethiopia
    (2) Caracas, Venezuela
    (3) New York City, USA
    (4) Karachi, Pakistan
    (5) Singapore, Singapore

43. In many developing countries there is a high urban growth rate and the urban population tends to be concentrated in large cities. Which of the following would help explain this fact?

    (1) Urban population growth rates in developed nations tend to be low.
    (2) Agricultural techniques are improving in developing countries.
    (3) Unsettled political conflicts may chase residents from cities.
    (4) There is a lack of work in rural areas in many developing countries.
    (5) Traditional societies sometimes resist social change.

44. Which of the following generalizations is supported by this table?

    (1) The rates and patterns of urban growth are different in every country.
    (2) Urbanization often negatively affects the quality of life of a country's inhabitants.
    (3) The average annual growth of cities in Asia is higher than that of cities in any other continent.
    (4) By the year 2015, urbanization rates will begin to fall in most countries.
    (5) Urban growth tends to promote industrialization.

Questions 45 through 48 refer to the following maps.

Sources of Immigration, 1871–1910

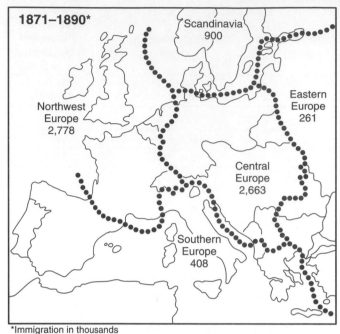

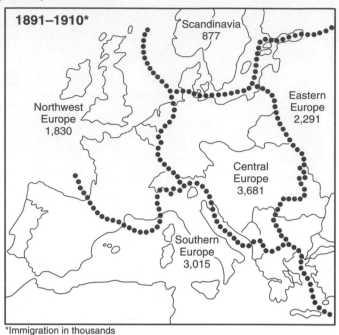

*Immigration in thousands

45. Which statement <u>best</u> explains why the ethnic make-up of many American cities changed considerably over a forty-year period?

  (1) Thousands of people from different cultural groups arrived in America from 1871 to 1910.
  (2) Immigration from Northwest Europe was highest between 1871 and 1891.
  (3) Limits on immigration quotas were established in 1914.
  (4) America really was the new land of milk and honey.
  (5) Immigrants from the Orient were arriving to work on the new cross-country railroad.

46. In 1910 New York City had half as many Italians as the city of Naples. What <u>best</u> explains this fact?

  (1) the decline of Naples as a major city
  (2) the fact that over 3,015,000 people had immigrated from Southern Europe
  (3) the fact that 3,681,000 people had immigrated from Central Europe
  (4) the map's evidence that 3,015 of the immigrants were Italian
  (5) the large Italian population of New York City today

47. Which of the following American monuments <u>best</u> represents the hopes of the immigrants?

  (1) the Lincoln Memorial
  (2) the Liberty Bell
  (3) the Statue of Liberty
  (4) the Washington Monument
  (5) Mount Rushmore

48. Which conclusion is supported by the pattern of immigration from 1891 to 1910?

  (1) Scandinavians were no longer interested in immigration.
  (2) Shortly after the turn of the century, language barriers forced many new arrivals into low-paying factory jobs.
  (3) By 1910 the immigrants had begun to adjust to their new surroundings.
  (4) Only Eastern Europeans were. interested in finding a new way of life
  (5) More and more European intellectuals were becoming aware of the opportunities that America offered.

49. You are traveling from Indianapolis, Indiana, to Sioux Falls, South Dakota. Your map shows the location of major cities, roads, and rivers. It shows direction and changes in elevation. It even indicates rest areas and campgrounds. Which of the following will you be unable to determine using your map?

   (1) if Chicago lies along your route
   (2) if you can stop for a picnic along the way
   (0) whether Sioux Falls is east or west of Rapid City
   (4) how many rivers you will be crossing
   (5) how far you will have to travel

50. Panama, a long, narrow country, links the North and South American continents. The Panama Canal crosses the width of Panama from one ocean to the other. Interestingly, the Pacific Ocean end of the canal lies east of the Atlantic Ocean end. What does this reveal about Panama's geographic position?

   (1) The Pacific Ocean is east of Panama.
   (2) The Atlantic Ocean is south of Panama.
   (3) Panama's length extends from north to south.
   (4) Panama's length extends from east to west.
   (5) Panama lies across the Equator.

Questions 51 and 52 refer to the following map and passage.

The deserts, or arid areas, of the world are expanding as a result of a process known as desertification. This occurs when humans living in semiarid areas near deserts overgraze the land and cut trees for firewood. With the vegetation gone, the soil is no longer protected from natural forces. In recent years, human activities in these areas have intensified, speeding up the process of desertification.

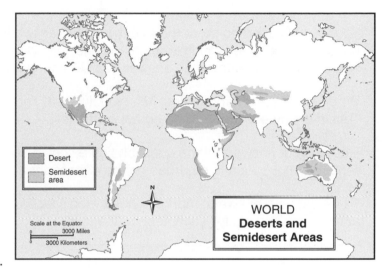

51. Which of the following has most likely led to the increased speed of desertification in some developing countries?

   (1) political instability
   (2) rapid population growth
   (3) expansion of economic activities to include manufacturing
   (4) low levels of education
   (5) reliance on imported manufactured goods

52. According to the map, which of the following continents has the largest desert area?

   (1) Africa
   (2) Australia
   (3) North America
   (4) South America
   (5) Eurasia

SOCIAL STUDIES

Directions

This Social Studies GED Simulated Test is intended to measure your knowledge of general social studies concepts.

The questions are based on short readings or on graphs, maps, charts, cartoons, and illustrations. Study the information given and then answer the questions that follow. Refer to the information as often as necessary in answering the questions.

You should spend no more than 70 minutes in answering the 50 questions on this test. Work carefully, but do not spend too much time on any one item. Do not skip any items. Make a reasonable guess when you are not sure of an answer. You will not be penalized for incorrect answers.

When time is up, mark the last item you finished. This will tell you whether you can finish the real GED Test in the time allowed. Then complete the test.

Record your answers to the questions on a copy of the answer sheet on page 110. Be sure that all required information is recorded on the answer sheet.

To record your answers, mark the numbered space on the answer sheet that corresponds to the answer you choose for each item on the test.

Example:

Early pioneers of the western frontier looked to settle on land that had adequate access to water. To ensure access to water, many early pioneers settled on land near which type of geographic feature?

(1) forests
(2) grasslands
(3) rivers
(4) glaciers
(5) oceans

The correct answer is rivers; therefore, answer space 3 should be marked on the answer sheet.

Do not rest the point of your pencil on the answer sheet while you are considering your answer. Make no stray or unnecessary marks. If you change an answer, erase your first mark completely. Mark only one answer for each question; multiple answers will be scored as incorrect. Do not fold or crease your answer sheet.

When you finish the test, use the Analysis of Performance Chart on page 71 to determine whether you are ready to take the real GED Test, and, if not, which skill areas need additional review.

Directions: Choose the <u>one best answer</u> to each question.

Questions 1 through 6 refer to the following map.

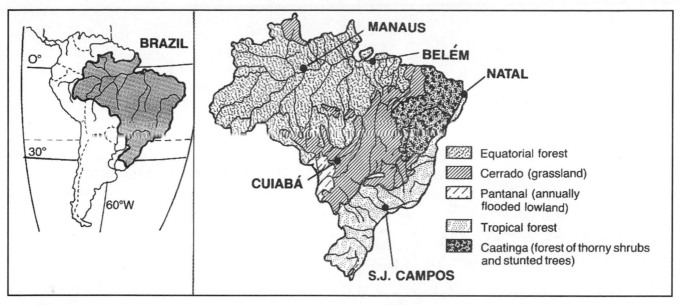

1. What can be discovered by using this map?

   (1) the major agricultural products of Brazil
   (2) Brazil's population densities
   (3) the location of mountains and plateaus
   (4) the location of mineral resources
   (5) major patterns of vegetation

2. According to the map, which is the least desirable area of Brazil?

   (1) the Equator
   (2) Natal
   (3) Manaus
   (4) approximately 15° S, 60° W
   (5) approximately 30° S, 70° W

3. Which of the following would <u>best</u> describe the climate of Brazil's equatorial forest?

   (1) cold and rainy
   (2) cold and snowy
   (3) mild and dry
   (4) mild and wet
   (5) hot and wet

4. Based on the map, which of the following describes Brazil?

   (1) the smallest South American country
   (2) the largest South American country
   (3) the largest Asian country
   (4) the smallest Asian country
   (5) a large island off the coast of South America

5. What conclusion do details of the map support?

   (1) Brazil is not a highly developed country.
   (2) Brazil has few natural resources.
   (3) Brazil's natural resources have not been fully exploited.
   (4) There are only five major cities in Brazil.
   (5) Brazil is larger than the United States.

6. One of the world's largest hydroelectric (water-driven) plants can be found in the Parana-Paraguay-Plata river complex in the southwest region of Brazil, west of Cuiabá. What information from the map suggests that this area is suitable for hydroelectric plants?

   (1) The equatorial forest surrounds the Amazon River.
   (2) The caatinga has vegetation that does not need much water.
   (3) The pantanal floods annually.
   (4) Tropical forests contain a rich abundance of wildlife.
   (5) The cerrado supports agriculture.

Question 7 refers to the following cartoon.

"LET'S NOT WORK SO HARD GROWING OUR OWN SAFE-TO-EAT VEGETABLES THAT WE BREATHE TOO MUCH OF THIS AIR."

7. This cartoon supports which of the following conclusions?

(1) Home gardens are not really worth the effort.
(2) Growing one's own safe-to-eat vegetables helps the overall environment.
(3) Individual efforts to combat environmental problems are threatened by even larger environmental ills.
(4) Growing safe-to-eat vegetables is more difficult than growing regular vegetables.
(5) Gardening is good exercise.

Question 8 refers to the following illustration.

The Far West.—shooting buffalo on the line of the Kansas-Pacific Railroad

8. Which of the following statements is best supported by this illustration from the late 1800s?

(1) Indians did not hunt buffalo.
(2) Buffalo were killed for food.
(3) Buffalo were killed as white civilization moved westward.
(4) Buffalo are extinct today.
(5) Buffalo are indigenous to Montana.

Questions 9 through 12 refer to the following passage.

In 1619 twenty Africans were brought to Virginia by a Dutch trading ship and exchanged for supplies. They were accepted as indentured servants to be freed from servitude after a specified time. But because they were so different in speech and appearance from the English settlers, these men and women were viewed only as a source of needed labor and were not freed after the time of indenture was over. By 1776 even such distinguished patriots as Washington and Jefferson ran their estates by using slave labor. However, despite his dependence on and recognition of the economic advantages of slavery, Jefferson was intellectually opposed to the institution and made arrangements to eventually free his own slaves.

9. What inference can be made from the passage?

   (1) The beginning of slavery in America was planned in advance.
   (2) The status of the English indentured servant was easily violated.
   (3) The twenty Africans were more than willing to work cheaply.
   (4) Slavery was well established by the time of the American Revolution.
   (5) Washington was morally unfit to be President.

10. "We hold these truths to be self-evident, that all men are created equal, that they are endowed by their Creator with certain unalienable Rights, that among these are Life, Liberty, and the pursuit of Happiness." from *The Declaration of Indpendence*

   Even though Jefferson may have had his slaves in mind when he wrote that all men are created equal, this principle was not generally thought of as applying to the black slaves. Which of the following is a likely explanation for this situation?

   (1) Washington disagreed with him.
   (2) Slaves had been regarded for too long as property rather than people.
   (3) Most slaves were women.
   (4) Jefferson had not yet freed his slaves.
   (5) Slavery existed only in Virginia.

11. Which of the following attitudes bears a resemblance to those of the Virginia colonials?

   (1) the German people ignoring the actions of Adolf Hitler
   (2) hippies being arrested for protesting against the Vietnam War
   (3) laws against child labor
   (4) women's suffrage movements continuing for so long without result
   (5) the prohibition of alcohol

12. Which of the following conclusions about the first President of the United States does the passage support?

   (1) He was against the institution of slavery.
   (2) He was a slave owner.
   (3) He was a hard man to work for.
   (4) He planned to free the slaves.
   (5) He was in favor of indentured servants.

Question 13 refers to the following passage.

Human population was ecologically insignificant for the first 2 million years of our existence. Only about 10 million humans inhabited the earth. With the advent of agricultural techniques, human populations began to increase rapidly. By the Christian Era, populations had reached some 200 million. They had more than doubled by 1650. During the first two millennia of the Christian Era, plagues and epidemics, often fed by immigration and trade, periodically wiped out large parts of populations worldwide. However, extraordinary population growth occurred during the twentieth century.

13. Which of the following provides the best explanation for the rise in population between 1930 and the present?

   (1) new medicines and no decrease in the birthrate
   (2) improved agricultural techniques
   (3) an increase in infant mortality
   (4) an increase in available water sources
   (5) improved communication and transportation

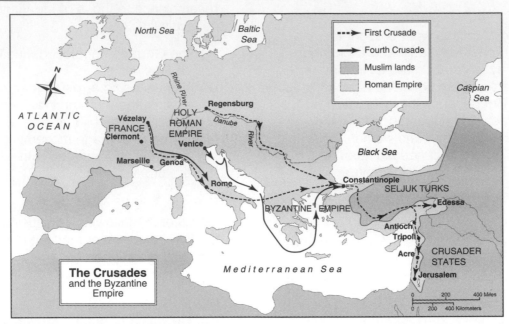

The Crusades were military campaigns by European Christian armies against Muslim territories, primarily as an attempt to capture Jerusalem and save it from "infidels." The Crusades took place from the eleventh through the fourteenth centuries. The First Crusade succeeded in temporarily occupying four Crusader States, from Antioch south to Jerusalem, but through infighting and Muslim resistance, these states were never consolidated. In 1204, during the Fourth Crusade, European armies sacked and savagely looted Constantinople. The victors installed a Flemish count as emperor and founded the Latin Empire of Constantinople, which came to an end in 1261 when Muslim troops re-entered the city. By that time, the power of the Latin emperors scarcely extended beyond the walls of the city. The Byzantine Empire was reconstituted, but faced threats from the West and from Turkey. Finally, in 1453, Constantinople was conquered by the Turks, who founded the Ottoman Empire. The Byzantine Empire was no more.

14. The Crusades are thought to have weakened the power of the Church in the West. Which of the following might have been a factor in this loss of power?

    (1) introduction of trade from Muslim lands
    (2) economic drain of military campaigns
    (3) loss of interest in religion
    (4) dependence on Venetian support
    (5) translation in 1143 of the Koran

15. Which of the following is an opinion rather than a fact about the Crusades?

    (1) Constantinople was recaptured by the Muslims in 1261.
    (2) The First, Second, and Third Crusades failed to dislodge the Byzantine Empire.
    (3) The Muslims conquered Constantinople.
    (4) The Crusades were a foolish military adventure.
    (5) The Ottoman Empire succeeded the Byzantine Empire.

16. Which of the following cities became a Crusader State, according to the passage and historical map?

    (1) Rome
    (2) Edessa
    (3) Tripoli
    (4) Constantinople
    (5) Venice

17. Which of the following is best supported by the passage?

    (1) The First Crusade made Jerusalem permanently a Crusader State.
    (2) The Crusaders were unable to "save" Jerusalem from the "infidels."
    (3) The Popes generally did not support the Crusades.
    (4) Constantinople was sacked.
    (5) The Crusades consolidated the Holy Roman Empire.

18. From the passage and map, which of the following might be concluded regarding the Second and Third Crusades?

   (1) Neither the Second nor Third Crusade succeeded.
   (2) There was no Second or Third Crusade.
   (3) Both the Second and Third Crusade succeeded in occupying Jerusalem.
   (4) The Second Crusade lasted 15 years.
   (5) The Third Crusade lasted 50 years.

Question 19 refers to the following graphs.

U.S. Farms, 1943–1999

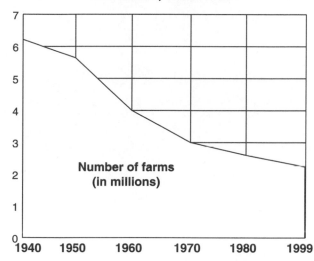

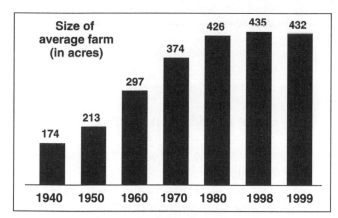

19. What conclusion about trends in farm ownership in the United States can be drawn from the statistics presented in these graphs?

   (1) Farms have gotten smaller.
   (2) Small farms are disappearing.
   (3) Farm size doubled from 1998 to 1999.
   (4) Farms have become unpopular.
   (5) The size of farms and the number of farms have no relation to each other.

Question 20 refers to the following graph.

Women in National Parliaments as of Jan.1, 1998
(by Region)

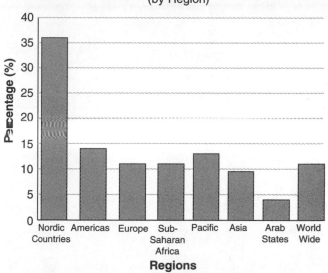

20. Which of the following conclusions can be supported by the information in the chart?

   (1) Women have gained political power in the last 10 years.
   (2) Women hold fewer parliamentary seats in sub-Saharan Africa than in Arab states.
   (3) There are fewer male members of parliaments in Nordic countries than in the Americas.
   (4) Citizens of Nordic countries believe more fervently in equality of the sexes than citizens of other regions.
   (5) The United States has many women in Congress.

21. This is a photograph of a worker in a textile factory in the early twentieth century. What change in U.S. law during this period attempted to prevent the situation depicted in the photograph?

    (1) establishment of a minimum wage
    (2) recognition of labor unions
    (3) creation of a social security system
    (4) institution of child labor laws
    (5) state-supported education

Question 22 refers to the following cartoon.

The Working "People."

22. Which of the following is implied in this cartoon from the early twentieth century?

    (1) Working people were pleased with their jobs.
    (2) People will usually follow a strong leader.
    (3) Some individuals profited at the expense of other people's labor.
    (4) Unions were the result of workers' dissatisfaction.
    (5) The construction industry was more profitable then than now.

Questions 23 through 26 refer to the following passage and table.

As barter is no longer a practical way for most people to get the items needed for modern living, many societies use some form of money as their major medium of exchange. The dollar is the basis for currency in the United States and is recognized in two forms, coins and paper. Because the dollar is accepted as a standard and has a value guaranteed by the federal government, dollar payments are accepted for both products and services. Because the government has declared paper money to represent an actual commodity (the gold reserve), paper money along with coins is called legal tender.

Gold Reserves of Central Banks and Governments
(in million fine troy ounces)

	1975	1985	1995	1996	1997	1998	1999
All countries	1,017.71	949.39	908.79	906.10	890.57	966.15	940.51
United States	242.71	262.65	261.70	261.66	261.64	261.61	261.67
Belgium	42.17	34.18	20.54	15.32	15.32	9.52	8.30
Canada	21.95	20.11	3.41	3.09	3.09	2.49	1.81
France	100.93	81.85	81.85	81.85	81.89	102.37	97.24
Germany*	117.61	95.18	95.18	95.18	95.18	118.98	111.52
Italy	82.48	66.67	66.67	66.67	66.67	83.36	78.83
Japan	21.11	24.33	24.23	24.23	24.23	24.23	24.23
Netherlands	54.33	43.94	34.77	34.77	27.07	33.83	31.57
Switzerland	83.20	83.28	83.28	83.28	83.28	83.26	83.28
United Kingdom	21.03	19.03	18.43	18.43	18.42	23.00	20.55

* West Germany prior to 1991

23. Which of the following can also be called legal tender?

   (1) a handwritten IOU
   (2) a verbal promise to repay a debt
   (3) a check written on an approved bank form
   (4) a receipt
   (5) a bank statement

24. Which of the following reasons best explains why barter has become impractical?

   (1) People no longer have the time to argue over the worth of an item.
   (2) Our society has become too complex to trade on an item-per-item basis.
   (3) People are easily cheated when they use the barter system.
   (4) Marketplaces have vanished from most cities.
   (5) Barter requires skills that we no longer have.

25. If the countries in the table were grouped into regions, which region probably holds the greatest amount of gold reserves?

   (1) North America
   (2) South America
   (3) the Middle East
   (4) Europe
   (5) the Pacific Rim

26. If the United States were to return to the "gold standard," as some economists propose, dollar bills would have a one-to-one correspondence with the actual gold held by the U.S. What would be the consequence of such an action?

   (1) There would be a limit on the number of bills printed.
   (2) People might begin trading with gold coins.
   (3) Banks would no longer accept bills as legal tender.
   (4) Trade might return to the barter system.
   (5) Dollar bills would lose value.

Questions 27 through 32 refer to the following chart and passage.

Organizational Chart, United Nations

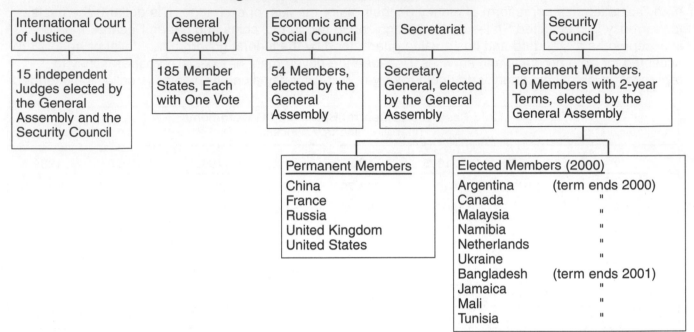

from the United Nations Charter
THE SECURITY COUNCIL
COMPOSITION (Article 23)

1. The Security Council shall consist of fifteen Members of the Untied Nations. The Republic of China, France, the Union of Soviet Socialist Republics, the United Kingdom of Great Britain and Northern Ireland, and the United States of America shall be permanent members of the Securtiy Council. The General Assembly shall elect ten other Members of the United Nations to be non-permanent members of the Security Council, due regard being specially paid, in the first instance to the contribution of Members of the United Nations to the maintenance of international peace and security and to the other purposes of the Organization, and also to equitable geographical distribution.

2. The non-permanent members of the Security Council shall be elected for a term of two years.... A retiring member shall not be eligible for immediate re-election.

VOTING (Article 27)

1. Each member of the Security Council shall have one vote.
2. Decisions of the Security Council on procedural matters shall be made by an affirmative vote of nine members.

3. Decision of the Security Council on all other matters shall be made by an affirmative vote of nine members including the concurring votes of the permanent members; provided that...a party to a dispute shall abstain from voting.

27. Which of the following countries will be ineligible to serve in the Security Council in 2001?

(1) Argentina
(2) Mali
(3) Tunisia
(4) China
(5) Bangladesh

28. If the United Kingdom votes against a nonprocedural matter in the Security Council, what will be the outcome?

(1) The proposition will pass only if nine other members support it.
(2) The matter will be sent back to the General Assembly for its consideration.
(3) The matter will be tabled (set aside for later consideration).
(4) The proposition will not pass.
(5) The United States will decide whether the proposition passes or not.

29. If the United States votes against a procedural matter in the Security Council, what will be the result?

    (1) It will definitely pass.
    (2) It will pass if nine other members support it.
    (3) The United States will veto the matter.
    (4) Only the United States can vote on procedural matters.
    (5) It will probably fail.

30. Assume that China and Russia are involved in a border dispute. According to the U.N. Charter, how must they vote in the Security Council?

    (1) They must concur.
    (2) They must vote to veto.
    (3) They must abstain.
    (4) They may vote their conscience.
    (5) The United States will vote in their place.

31. In order to become part of the Security Council as a non-permanent voting member, which of the following requirements must be met?

    (1) The country must be a member state but not one of the Permanent Members.
    (2) The country must be from Central America.
    (3) The country must have a representative in the Economic and Social Council.
    (4) The country must have served on the Security Council in the last term.
    (5) The country must have two votes in the General Assembly.

32. Which of the following groups of countries would be unlikely to serve during the same term in the Security Council?

    (1) The United States, China, France
    (2) Argentina, Namibia, Malaysia
    (3) Switzerland, India, Uruguay
    (4) Belgium, Denmark, Germany
    (5) China, Russia, Bangladesh

Question 33 refers to the following table.

Voter Turnout in Presidential Elections, 1933-96

Candidates	Voter Participation (% of voting-age population)
1932 Roosevelt-Hoover	52.4
1936 Roosevelt-Landon	56.0
1940 Roosevelt-Willkie	58.9
1944 Roosevelt-Dewey	56.0
1010 Truman-Dewey	51.1
1952 Stevenson-Eisenhower	61.6
1956 Stevenson-Eisenhower	59.3
1960 Kennedy-Nixon	62.8
1964 Johnson-Goldwater	61.9
1968 Humphrey-Nixon	60.9
1972 McGovern-Nixon	55.2[1]
1976 Carter-Ford	53.5
1980 Carter-Reagan	54.0
1984 Mondale-Reagan	53.1
1988 Dukakis-Bush	50.2
1992 Clinton-Bush-Perot	55.9
1996 Clinton-Dole-Perot	49.0

(1) The sharp drop in 1972 followed the expansion of eligibility with the enfranchisement of 18- to 20-year-olds.

33. Which of the following is supported by information in the table?

    (1) The fact that Roosevelt ran again in 1944 prompted an increase in voter turnout.
    (2) Voter participation increased steadily from 1956 to 1968.
    (3) The highest percentage of voter turnout was a result of Kennedy running for President.
    (4) The percentage of voter participation has remained constant since 1932.
    (5) The percentage of voter participation dropped quite a bit when 18- to 20-year-olds were given the right to vote.

Question 34 refers to the following graph.

Elderly in the Labor Force, 1890–1900
(labor force participation rate; figs. for 1910 not available)

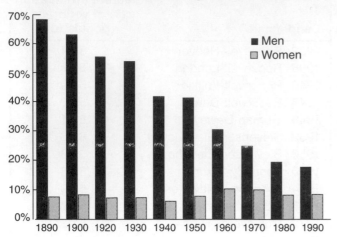

Question 36 refers to the following graph.

U.S. Unemployment Rates 1987–1999

34. In a comparison of elderly women to elderly men, what long-term trend can be seen in the graph?

  (1) Both groups have seen a steady decline in workforce participation.
  (2) Both groups have seen a steady increase in workforce participation.
  (3) Women have increased while men have decreased in participation.
  (4) Men have increased while women have decreased in participation.
  (5) No long-term trend is discernable.

36. If unemployment rates relate to the health of the economy, what can you infer from this graph?

  (1) The U.S. economy is not very healthy.
  (2) Economic growth leads to high levels of unemployment.
  (3) The early 1990s was a period of economic recession.
  (4) Many women joined the workforce in the 1990s.
  (5) It was hard to find a job in 1999.

35. In a totalitarian government, the leaders recognize no one else's authority and use the government to control almost all aspects of civilian life. There is only one political party, and policies are often imposed by force. Which of the following would be opposed by a totalitarian government?

  (1) governmental control of the mass media
  (2) centralized armed forces
  (3) room for Communist theory
  (4) free elections
  (5) government bureaucracy

Question 37 refers to the following cartoon.

By David Seavey, USA TODAY. Copyright 1989, USA TODAY. Reprinted with permission.

37. What is the main idea of the cartoon?

(1) Many criminals are back on the streets because the prisons cannot hold all those convicted.
(2) Rehabilitation programs in prisons are not effective.
(3) Prison rehabilitation programs are working so well that many convicts are getting out on parole.
(4) Too many innocent people are being sentenced to jail terms.
(5) Prison conditions are so bad that inmates are rioting in the streets.

38. In 1981, a professor announced to her class that the 52 American hostages in Iran had been released after 444 days in captivity. Her students had no idea what she was talking about. In despair, she assigned students to read news articles and watch television newscasts in addition to the usual homework. The teacher was upset that her students placed so little value on which of the following?

(1) doing their studies
(2) the right to freedom
(3) international politics
(4) television as a source of news
(5) American lives

Question 39 refers to the following passage.

In economics, the law of supply and demand is a basic factor in determining price. According to this law, price is determined by the amount of goods or services available for sale (supply) and the amount of those goods or services purchasers want to buy (demand). Theoretically, when supply exceeds demand, prices will go down, and conversely, when demand exceeds supply, prices will go up.

39. Which of the following is supported by this information?

(1) Lowering prices will lower demand.
(2) Lowering prices will increase demand.
(3) Raising prices will increase demand.
(4) Raising prices will not change demand.
(5) Lowering prices will not change demand.

Question 40 refers to the following graph.

U.S. Resident Pleasure Travel Volume, 1994–1999
(in millions of person-trips of 50 miles or more, one-way)

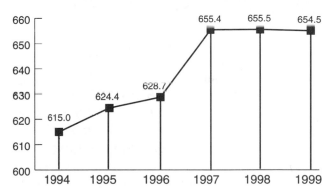

40. What conclusion about U.S. tourism might be drawn from the graph?

(1) Tourism is economically unstable.
(2) Tourism has abandoned the domestic market.
(3) Tourism increased in the five years covered by the graph.
(4) Tourism is not dependent on the general economy.
(5) Tourism is in permanent decline.

Questions 41 through 45 refer to the following passage and map.

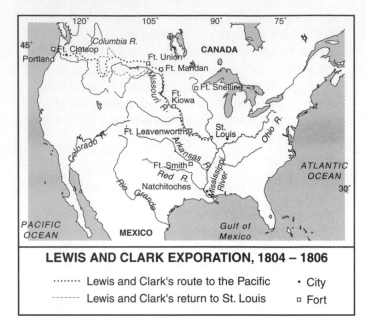

LEWIS AND CLARK EXPORATION, 1804 – 1806

········· Lewis and Clark's route to the Pacific   • City

 Lewis and Clark's return to St. Louis   ▫ Fort

In 1803, after the Louisiana Purchase, President Thomas Jefferson persuaded Congress to appropriate funds for a voyage of discovery to seek out a Northwest Passage. Long dreamed of by explorers and politicians, the Passage, it was hoped, would extend continuously from the Mississippi to the Pacific Ocean. Meriwether Lewis and William Clark were chosen to lead the expedition. The plan was to begin in St. Louis and travel up the Missouri River as far as the Rocky Mountains by the winter of 1804–1805. Then, in the spring, the explorers would cross the "short portage" from the Missouri to the Columbia River and thence to the Pacific, reaching that great ocean by spring of 1805.

Difficult though the initial journey was, all went according to plan for the first leg of the trip. The party spent the winter of 1804–1805 with the Mandan Indians, in North Dakota. When they left in April, the party had acquired the invaluable Shoshoni guide Sacagawea. Her perserverance and knowledge insured the completion of the voyage.

Still, even with Sacagawea's assistance, the explorers were unable to find a continuous water passage. After torturous false starts and dead ends, coupled with crippling overland journeys, the party finally reached the Columbia River in November 1805. After a winter on the Pacific shore, near present-day Portland, the party began its return trip. In an attempt to find the missing passage, the party split in two. Although the two parties met again on the Missouri, neither had discovered the mythical continuous water route. However, the "Corps of Discovery," as it was called, had managed to map much of the vast lands that became our American West.

41. Of what value would a Northwest Passage have been to politicians and business interests?

   (1) It might serve to unify the country.
   (2) It would encourage Congress to sell the Louisiana Purchase.
   (3) A similar passage might be discovered in the Southeast.
   (4) Northeastern fur traders wanted to bring their wares to Portland.
   (5) European settlers in Portland wanted to take trips back east.

42. What misconception on the part of Lewis and Clark may have contirubuted to some of the difficulties they encountered?

   That

   (1) the Pacific Ocean was much closer
   (2) they could reach the Rocky Mountains before winter
   (3) there was only a short portage between the Missouri and Columbia Rivers
   (4) they could follow an existing map of the Northwest
   (5) Louisiana bordered on the Pacific Ocean

43. Why might Lewis and Clark have planned to winter at the point furthest upstream on the Missouri River?

   (1) Winter is the best time for travel.
   (2) Spring and summer are the best time to travel.
   (3) Sacagawea recommended wintering there.
   (4) Otherwise, the explorers would run out of materials.
   (5) They had already found the Northwest Passage.

44. What is the <u>most likely</u> reason St. Louis was chosen as the starting point for this expedition?

    (1) It was on the same latitude as Washington, D.C.
    (2) It was located at the juncture of the Mississippi and Missouri Rivers.
    (3) It was designated the capital of the Louisiana Purchase.
    (4) It was already a great railway center.
    (5) It was a center of learning and higher education.

45. Why did Lewis and Clark fail to find the Northwest Passage?

Because

    (1) Sacagawea did not know the way
    (2) the Mississippi does not connect with the Missouri
    (3) the Columbia River does not go to the Pacific Ocean
    (4) they did not have a map
    (5) a continuous water passage does not exist

46. The United Nations is an international organization designed to maintain international peace and to encourage cultural and economic exchange between nations. What does the existence of such an organization assume about its member nations?

    (1) They are in agreement on all vital issues.
    (2) They are culturally similar.
    (3) They will try to work out their political differences.
    (4) They expect another world war.
    (5) They have economic resources that they are willing to share.

Question 47 refers to the following table.

Canada: Population by Province / Territory		
Provinces/Territories	Area (sq. mi.)	Population (1996 cen.)
Alberta	255,287	2,696,826
British Columbia	365,948	3,724,500
Manitoba	250,947	1,113,898
New Brunswick	28,355	738,133
Newfoundland	156,649	551,792
Nova Scotia	21,425	909,282
Ontario	412,581	10,753,573
Prince Edward Island	2,185	134,557
Quebec	594,860	7,138,795
Saskatchewan	251,866	990,237
Northwest Territories	503,951	39,672
Yukon Territory	186,661	30,766
Nunavut	818,959	24,730

47. Which of the following is supported by information in the table?

    (1) Canada has a wide diversity of population densities
    (2) Quebec is the biggest province in Canada
    (3) The biggest province in Canada also has the largest population.
    (4) The most populous province of Canada is the second largest.
    (5) Only two Canadian provinces have populations over 1 million.

48. A percentage of campaign funds for congressional candidates comes from political action committees (PACs), which represent special interest groups.
What might explain why there are many PACs?

    (1) There are many special interests.
    (2) Elected officials that PACs support in turn support the special interests.
    (3) Members of Congress only want their money.
    (4) They represent the democratic interests of many people.
    (5) Most of their negotiations are done in secret.

Question 49 refers to the following table.

Universities of Venezuela

University	Location	Year Founded	Enrollment (1990)
Andes, University of the	Mérida	1785	34,300
Andrés Bello Catholic University	Caracas	1953	11,600
Carabobo, University of	Valencia	1852	44,700
East, University of the	Cumaná	1958	32,100
Santa Maria University	Caracas	1953	c. 4,500
Simón Bolivar University	Caracas	1970	10,000
Venezuela, Central University of	Caracas	1721	45,000
Zulia, University of	Maracaibo	1891	47,600

49. Which of the following inferences is supported by information in the table?

(1) Venezuela has a high rate of literacy.
(2) Caracas was established by the eighteenth century.
(3) Education is well supported in Venezuela.
(4) Venezuela's university system resembles that of Spain.
(5) Students in Venezuela prefer modern universities.

Question 50 refers to the following cartoon.

HANK MCCLURE Courtesy Lawton Constitution. Reprinted by permission of the cartoonist.

50. What does the man's request show that he most likely believes?

(1) An economic upturn is on the way.
(2) The economy will improve in nations other than the United States.
(3) Newspapers are good sources of information.
(4) There is little chance of an economic recovery reaching the poor.
(5) Up-to-date news about the economy is useful in day-to-day life.

SOCIAL STUDIES

The chart below will help you determine your strengths and weaknesses on the content and skill areas of the GED Social Studies Test. Use the Answers and Explanations starting on page 103 to check your answers on the test.

Directions: Circle the number of each item that you answered correctly on the Simulated GED Test A. Count the number of items you answered correctly in each column. Write the amount in the Total Correct space of each column. (For example, If you answered 8 U. S. History items correctly, place the number 8 in the blank before out of 13.) Complete this process for the remaining columns.

Count the number of items you answered correctly in each row. Write that amount in the Total Correct space of each row. (For example, in the Comprehension row, write the number correct in the blank before out of 10.) Complete this process for the remaining rows.

Content / Cognitive Level	United States History (Unit 1)	World History (Unit 2)	Civics and Government (Unit 3)	Economics (Unit 4)	Geography (Unit 5)	Total Correct
Comprehension	12, **22**, **37**, **42***		**31***	**25***, 34, 36	1, 4	_____ out of 10
Application	**8**, 11, **45***	**14***	**30***	21, **23***, **26***		_____ out of 8
Analysis	9, 10, **41***, **43***, **44***	13, **15***, **16***, **18***	**27***, **28***, **29*** 32*, 39, 46, 48	19, **24***, 40	2, 6	_____ out of 21
Evaluation	33	**17***, 20	7, 35, 38	50	3, 5, 47, 49	_____ out of 11
Total Correct	____ out of 13	____ out of 7	____ out of 12	____ out of 10	____ out of 8	Total Correct: _____ out of 50 1–40 = You need more review. 41–50 = Congratulations! You're ready.

Boldface items indicate questions that include graphics.
Boldface items with an asterisk (*) indicate questions with a combination of a graphic and a prose passage.

If you answered fewer than 41 questions correctly, determine which areas are hardest for you. Go back to the *Steck-Vaughn GED Social Studies* book and review the content in those specific areas.

In the parentheses beneath the heading, the units tell you where you can find specific instruction about that area in the *Steck-Vaughn GED Social Studies* book. Also refer to the chart on page 3 of this book.

SOCIAL STUDIES

Directions

This Social Studies GED Simulated Test is intended to measure your knowledge of general social studies concepts.

The questions are based on short readings or on graphs, maps, charts, cartoons, and illustrations. Study the information given and then answer the questions that follow. Refer to the information as often as necessary in answering the questions.

You should spend no more than 70 minutes in answering the 50 questions on this test. Work carefully, but do not spend too much time on any one item. Do not skip any items. Make a reasonable guess when you are not sure of an answer. You will not be penalized for incorrect answers.

When time is up, mark the last item you finished. This will tell you whether you can finish the real GED Test in the time allowed. Then complete the test.

Record your answers to the questions on a copy of the answer sheet on page 110. Be sure that all required information is recorded on the answer sheet.

To record your answers, mark the numbered space on the answer sheet that corresponds to the answer you choose for each item on the test.

Example:

Early pioneers of the western frontier looked to settle on land that had adequate access to water. To ensure access to water, many early pioneers settled on land near which type of geographic feature?

(1) forests
(2) grasslands
(3) rivers
(4) glaciers
(5) oceans

The correct answer is rivers; therefore, answer space 3 should be marked on the answer sheet.

Do not rest the point of your pencil on the answer sheet while you are considering your answer. Make no stray or unnecessary marks. If you change an answer, erase your first mark completely. Mark only one answer for each question; multiple answers will be scored as incorrect. Do not fold or crease your answer sheet.

When you finish the test, use the Performance Analysis Chart on page 88 to determine whether you are ready to take the real GED Test, and, if not, which skill areas need additional review.

Directions: Choose the one best answer to each question.

Question 1 refers to the following politcal cartoon.

Michael Ramirez. Copley News Service.

1. Which of the following best explains what the cartoonist foresees for today's workers?

   (1) a bankrupt social security system
   (2) an increase of natural disasters
   (3) inadequate education
   (4) an abundance of pension funds
   (5) early retirement

Question 2 refers to the following political cartoon.

2. What does the cartoon suggest?

   (1) that racism is part of American culture
   (2) that Uncle Sam is late for dinner
   (3) that racism cannot occur in America
   (4) that racism is caused by hunger
   (5) that termites ruin American homes

Question 3 refers to the following map.

Aquifers in the United States

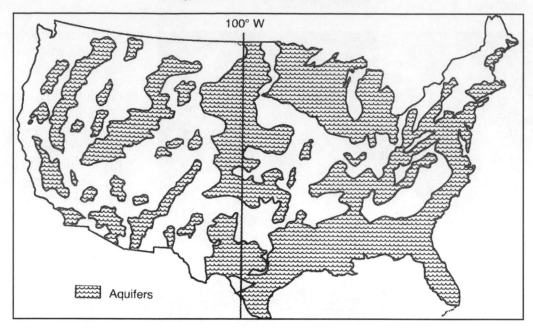

100° W

Aquifers

3. The shaded areas of the map represent aquifers, reservoirs of underground water. Which of the following is true about the 100°W meridian?

(1) It runs across the driest part of the nation
(2) It essentially acts as a boundary between the wet and dry sections of the United States.
(3) It runs across an area where there are no aquifers.
(4) It follows the course of the Mississippi River.
(5) It acts as a division between saltwater and freshwater reservoirs.

Question 4 refers to the following passage.

Acid rain, which damages plant and animal life, is the result of toxic chemicals combining with water particles in the air. Many Canadians blame the production of the acid rain that is affecting their environment on American industry.

4. What does this accusation suggest about pollution problems?

(1) They can affect relations between friendly nations.
(2) They can be solved through a mutual effort.
(3) They can be blamed completely on United States factories.
(4) They affect Canadians but not Americans.
(5) They have nothing to do with Canadian factories.

AXIS EXPANSION IN EUROPE 1942

- The Axis and it's allies
- The Allies
- Axis occupied or controlled
- Vichy
- Neutral States
- - - - Start of German advance into U.S.S.R.
- —— Farthest extent of German advance into U.S.S.R.
- • City

By 1940, Hitler's Germany was preeminent in Europe. Belgium, Holland, Denmark, Poland, Norway, and tiny Luxembourg suffered invasions and occupation. Finally, on June 14, Hitler's armies invaded Paris and France was soon divided between an occupied North and a collaborationist South, headed by Marshal Petain.

Secure in domination of Europe, with only Britain offering substantial resistance, Hitler turned to the east, opening up a second front. Stalin, who had joined Hitler in a nonagression pact, was surprised to find his troops facing the highly advanced technology of the German troops. The Nazis marched quickly into Soviet territory, reaching the outskirts of Moscow and Leningrad by September 1941. Stalin, belatedly rallying his people to action, called for active resistance. By December, the Red Army was able to counterattack along the entire front. It failed to stop the Germans only in the south, where the German advance continued unabated until September 1942.

In the north, Nazis held Leningrad under siege, inflicting starvation in freezing conditions and cruel death on nearly one-third of the citizens. Finally, in 1944, the siege lifted and the Red Army pursued the Nazis back into Poland and further west. The Second Front had failed, and along with it the ability of the German Army to retain its hold on Europe.

5. Which of the following might explain why German troops advanced very quickly on the Soviet Union?

   (1) The weather was conducive to the German action.
   (2) Stalin's nonagression pact with Hitler left his country unprepared for the possibility of war with Germany.
   (3) Hitler's troops advanced under cover of darkness.
   (4) Germans and Russians were historically allies.
   (5) Hitler had never invaded a country previously.

6. As the German advance stalled along the Russian front in autumn 1941, what factor might have worked in the Soviets' favor to help keep the Germans at bay?

    (1) American assistance
    (2) Stalin's leadership
    (3) the coming winter
    (4) Finland's neutrality
    (5) the strong Soviet economy

7. By 1942, which of the following European countries remained in the Allied camp?

    (1) Spain
    (2) Greece
    (3) Sweden
    (4) Iceland
    (5) Ireland

8. Which of the following is supported by information in the passage and the map?

    (1) Marshal Petain was responsible for saving Stalingrad.
    (2) The Battle of Leningrad was won by the Nazis.
    (3) The battle of Stalingrad was a stalemate.
    (4) Soviet troops must have held at Stalingrad, because no German troops advanced beyond this point.
    (5) German troops took both Leningrad and Stalingrad.

9. According to the map, what stance did Italy take during the war?

    (1) It was conquered by Germany.
    (2) It was neutral.
    (3) It was part of the Allied forces.
    (4) It was part of the Axis forces and was not conquered by Germany.
    (5) It had been conquered previously by Britain.

Question 10 refers to the following photograph and historical document.

Library of Congress

Amendment XXI
Repeal of Amendment XVIII.

1. The eighteenth article of amendment to the Constitution of the United States is hereby repealed.

2. The transportation or importation into any State, Territory, or possession of the United States for delivery or use therein of intoxicating liquors, in violation of the laws thereof, is hereby prohibited…

10. Which of the following statements is supported by the photograph and document?

    (1) Women were voting in too few numbers.
    (2) Citizens were taking unfair advantage of their free speech rights.
    (3) Repeal of the 18th Amendment had broad-based popular support.
    (4) Liquor could only be consumed by women.
    (5) Automobiles played a major role in the passage of the 18th Amendment.

Questions 11 through 15 refer to the following passage.

The Great Depression had an impact on German businesses. German industry, despite all its merits, had a fundamental weakness. It was built on credit. It functioned well as long as Germans could borrow without immediate repayment. Any retraction of promised materials or credit would cause a violent reaction throughout the country's industry. The sudden recall of short-term loans began to endanger the continued operation of numerous plants. Foreign tariffs and quotas had devastating repercussions because most German firms had no reserves on which to draw. When the American stock market crashed in 1929, American agencies began recalling their loans. This had a paralyzing effect on Germany. As the depression deepened, markets were cut off even as demands for repayment increased.

In 1931 the Viennese bank, Kreditanstalt, failed. This prevented German banks from recalling their major deposits with that institution. The widespread bankruptcy and economic confusion which resulted in turn produced massive unemployment.

In 1933 newly appointed Chancellor Adolf Hitler created employment for 7 million people by ignoring the principles of laissez-faire. He sent the unemployed to farms and factories, whether they were needed or not. He drafted the remainder of the unemployed into the military. Within a year and a half, the Nazi government had total control of labor and industry and the German people.

11. Why did German businesses go bankrupt?

   (1) They could not repay loans.
   (2) The American stock market crashed.
   (3) Foreign tariffs increased.
   (4) Materials were no longer available.
   (5) They were poorly managed.

12. How did the American stock market crash of 1929 affect German exports?

   (1) Markets for German goods fell.
   (2) Prices increased for German exports.
   (3) It raised American competition.
   (4) It lowered the quality of exports.
   (5) It changed the German tariff structure.

13. Which of the following best explains the shaky condition of the German economy at the time of the Great Depression?

   (1) the fairly recent adoption of cost-saving industrial techniques
   (2) the reliance on credit
   (3) the split of Germany into East and West
   (4) the stability of the Viennese bank
   (5) the stock market crash

14. Which opinion does the passage support?

   (1) Banks can't be trusted.
   (2) Buying stocks will lead to disaster.
   (3) Whoever controls the economy controls the nation.
   (4) Businesses should never borrow money.
   (5) Principles of laissez-faire are worthless.

15. What feelings might Americans have had about the Viennese bank failure?

   (1) distrust of Swiss bank accounts
   (2) worry about the apparent weakness of savings and loan institutions
   (3) trust in only American banks and American currency
   (4) have both savings and checking accounts
   (5) conduct business through lawyers

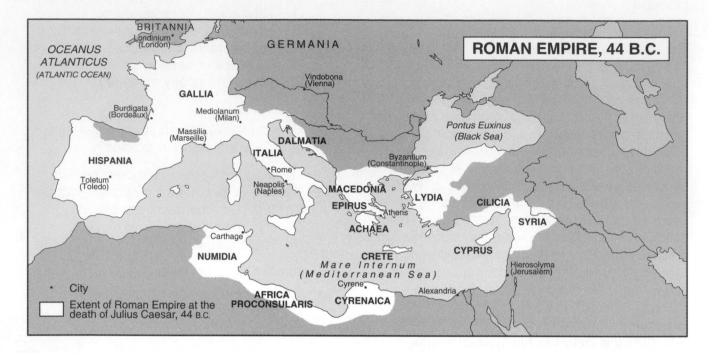

Although in 509 B.C. a Roman Republic succeeded the monarchy that had ruled Rome since its founding, the Republic did not originally represent all people. It was constituted as an aristocracy, with its Senate drawn from the upper class (the patricians). The common people (the plebians) were effectively disenfranchised. The Senate elected two Consuls, who headed the Senate (as a prime minister might today). In the early 5th century B.C., the Roman plebeians revolted. The Senate was reformed to allow plebeian representatives—called Tribunes—into the government. Plebeians gained even more power when a ban forbidding intermarriage between the classes was lifted in 445 B.C. Laws passed by the assembly of plebeians (called Plebecites) were accepted as binding on patricians and plebeians alike in 287 B.C. The Republic as constituted remained in place for over two centuries. For a short time, just before Julius Caesar's reign, franchise was extended to all Italians. However, any political participation was restricted to male citizens and was denied inhabitants of Rome's colonies. Political chaos in the first century B.C. resulted in the dissolution of the Republic under Julius Caesar and his nephew Augustus. The Senate effectively conceded power to Augustus in 42 B.C., conferring on him the honor of chief military commander—Imperium, from which we derive the word Emperor.

Democracy:	government conducted directly or indirectly by citizens
Dictatorship:	government conducted by the rule of a single person
Oligarchy:	literally "rule by few"
Republic:	government conducted by representatives of citizens

16. After the fifth century B.C., how did Rome's Republic differ from a direct democracy?

(1) People voted their class interests.
(2) Only the rich could vote.
(3) Citizens voted through representatives.
(4) Tribunes voted their conscience.
(5) Plebeians could not vote.

17. Which of the following cities would have enjoyed some measure of representation immediately preceding Julius Ceasar's reign?

(1) Athens
(2) Neapolis
(3) Londinium
(4) Cyrene
(5) Vindobona

18. What city lay outside Roman domination in 44 B.C.?

    (1) Carthage
    (2) Londinium
    (3) Massilia
    (4) Burdigata
    (5) Toletum

19. Under the "patrician republic" of early Rome, what form of government did the citizens of Rome enjoy?

    (1) monarchy
    (2) democracy
    (3) oligarchy
    (4) indirect democracy
    (5) dictatorship

Question 20 refers to the following table and passage.

Colonial American Population Estimates (in round numbers)

Year	Population	Year	Population
1610	350	1700	250,900
1620	2,300	1710	331,700
1630	4,600	1720	466,200
1640	26,600	1730	629,400
1650	50,400	1740	905,600
1660	75,100	1750	1,170,800
1670	111,900	1760	1,593,600
1680	151,500	1770	2,148,100
1690	210,400	1780	2,780,400

During the colonial era in America, the European population (and, indeed, the Native American population) could only be estimated given the lack of a systematized census. Not until 1790, after the establishment of the union, did a true national census take place.

20. Which of the following is supported by information in the table and passage?

    (1) Population was subject to the effects of disease.
    (2) Population showed a steady rise.
    (3) Population reveals the effects of emigration to other lands.
    (4) No trend is discernable.
    (5) Population was carefully counted.

Question 21 refers to the following photograph and quotation.

"Mistakes were made. I take full responsibility."

21. The incident known as Watergate precipitated the resignation of which of the following former U.S. Presidents shown in the photo?

    (1) John F. Kennedy
    (2) Richard Nixon
    (3) Ronald Reagan
    (4) George Bush
    (5) Bill Clinton

Question 22 refers to the following table.

Question 24 refers to the following timeline.

Table of Ethnicity/Race
Canada
(figures from 1986 census)

Ethnicity/Race	Percent
British	40
French	27
Other European	20
Indigenous Indian and Inuit	1.5
Other, mostly Asian	15

Ninth Century Feudal Europe

800	Charlemagne crowned Emperor
809	Death of Harun-al-Rashid (Baghdad)
825–870	Viking invasions of Ireland and England
827	Moslems establish themselves in Sicily
843	Treaty of Verdun; division of Carolingian Empire
845	Vikings attack Frankish Kingdom
858–886	Patriarchate of Photius in Constantinople
862	Vikings (Northmen) in Russia; Rurik in Novgorod
ca. 862	Introduction of Christianity among Slavs (St. Cyril and Methodius)
870	Treaty of Mersen; Charlemagne's Empire redivided
871–899	Reign of Alfred the Great in England
885	Vikings at the gates of Paris

22. Which of the following statements is supported by the information in the table?

    (1) The French comprise a large minority of the Canadian population.
    (2) Canada has the largest Chinese population in North America.
    (3) Canadians of British descent live mainly in western Canada.
    (4) The Inuit are the largest indigenous minority in Canada.
    (5) English and French are spoken in Canada.

23. In the mid-1800s, the American people believed that our country had a manifest destiny, a goal of becoming a world power. Part of the dream was to include all the land to the Pacific Ocean in the United States. Which of the following events is evidence of the reality of manifest destiny?

    (1) A dispute occurred between England and the United States over ownership of the Oregon Territory.
    (2) President Polk acquired the territories of Oregon, Texas, and California.
    (3) Henry Clay lost the 1844 presidential election.
    (4) Texas declared independence from Spain in 1836 and became the Lone Star Republic.
    (5) Marcus Whitman led a thousand people westward on the Oregon Trail.

24. According to the chart, which of the following was a trend in ninth century Europe?

    (1) Islamic influence expands.
    (2) The Vikings sail to America.
    (3) Large parts of the Mediterranean are invaded by ship.
    (4) Christianity is introduced into new territories.
    (5) The Vikings invade various European countries.

Question 25 refers to the following graph.

Percentate of U.S. Population That Is Foreign-Born, 1900–1999

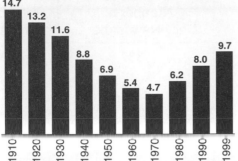

14.7 13.2 11.6 8.8 6.9 5.4 4.7 6.2 8.0 9.7

1910 1920 1930 1940 1950 1960 1970 1980 1990 1999

25. According to this graph, which of the following is <u>most likely</u> to occur in the year 2010?

The percentage of foreign-born Americans:

(1) will decrease somewhat
(2) will stay the same
(3) will drop to 4.7
(4) will increase somewhat
(5) will double the rate of 1980

Question 26 refers to the following cartoon.

Cartoon by Steve Nease.

26. Which of the following can be inferred from this Canadian editorial cartoon?

(1) Canadians have good healthcare.
(2) The Canadian tax burden is high.
(3) Budget surpluses always raise taxes.
(4) Politicians always raise taxes.
(5) Mining is an important Canadian industry.

Question 27 refers to the following table and passage.

NCAA Championship Sports Participation, 1981–1999		
Year	Women	Percent change* Women
1981–82	64,390	
1986–87	89,640	39.2
1991–92	94,920	5.9
1995–96	125,268	32.0
1990–97	129,295	0.2
1997–98	133,376	3.2
1998–99	145,832	9.3

* Percent change from previous year shown.

In 1972, Congress passed Title IX of the Education Amendments Act. This action prohibited discrimination against women in sports activities in all schools that receive federal aid. In primary and secondary schools, girls began to participate in large numbers. Before 1971, only 300,000 girls participated in high-school sports. By 1998 that number grew to 2.7 million.

27. Why might the table show large gains in women's participation in the mid 1980's?

(1) College women decided that sports was healthy.
(2) Fewer men participated those years.
(3) Title IX had been in place for a generation.
(4) More money was available at the college level.
(5) The NCAA promoted women's sports.

Question 28 refers to the following graphs.

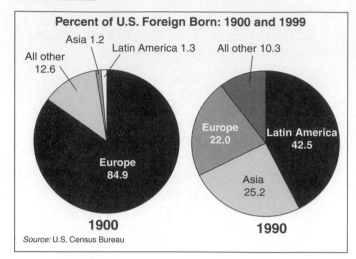

Percent of U.S. Foreign Born: 1900 and 1999

Asia 1.2
Latin America 1.3
All other 12.6
All other 10.3

Europe 84.9

1900

Europe 22.0
Latin America 42.5
Asia 25.2

1990

Source: U.S. Census Bureau

28. If any language can be said to be the second language of the United States, it is Spanish.

What evidence from the graphs above support this statement?

(1) the increase in immigrants from Latin America
(2) the decrease of immigrants from England
(3) the increase of immigrants from Asia
(4) the change in number of immigrants
(5) the proximity of Mexico to the U.S.

Question 29 refers to the following table.

| Income group | 1999 | | 1977 | |
	Average income	Share of all income (percent)	Average income	Share of all income (percent)
Lowest fifth	$8,800	4.2%	$10,000	5.7%
Second fifth	20,000	9.7	22,100	11.5
Middle fifth	31,400	14.7	32,400	16.4
Fourth fifth	45,100	21.3	42,600	22.8
Highest fifth	102,300	50.4	74,000	44.2
Top 1%	515,600	12.9	234,700	7.3

Average After-Tax Income in 1999 and 1977

29. Which of the following might account for the changes from 1977 to 1999?

(1) an increase in sales tax
(2) a rise in property tax rates
(3) a rise in the minimum wage
(4) a lowering of tax rates on high-income households
(5) a lowering of the earned income credit for low income families

Question 30 refers to the following chart.

Year	Number of Daily Newspapers	Total Daily Circulation
1860	387	1,478,000
1870	574	2,602,000
1880	971	3,566,000
1890	1,610	8,387,000
1900	2,226	15,102,000

American Newspapers 1860–1900

30. Which of the following might best explain the increase in number of newspapers published between 1860 and 1900?

(1) the founding of the American Library Association in 1876
(2) a substantial increase in literacy in the United States from 1860 to 1900
(3) a growing public interest in sensationalism
(4) a decrease in college enrollment
(5) the establishment of 15 graduate schools by the year 1900

31. The fixed exchange rate is the agreement between nations about what the official trading rate of their currencies will be. National banks can then buy and sell international currency in the world money market. Which of the following does the fixed exchange rate explain?

(1) the success of international banking
(2) why an American dollar and a Canadian dollar are often worth different amounts
(3) why rich people put their savings in Swiss bank accounts
(4) the fluctuation of the rate of inflation
(5) why Russian businesses want to sell goods to the United States

Questions 32 through 35 refer to the following chart and passage.

Estimated World Energy Consumption and Carbon Emissions, 1990–2020

Region	Energy consumption (quadrillon btu)			Carbon emissions (million metric tons)		
	1990	2010	2020	1990	2010	2020
Industrialized Nations[1]	182.8	238.7	259.9	2,850	3,563	3,928
Eastern Europe/Former Soviet Union	76.4	63.0	75.7	1,337	992	1,151
Developing nations						
Asia[2]	51.4	126.4	172.6	1,067	2,479	3,380
Middle East[3]	13.1	26.2	34.3	229	422	552
Africa	9.3	15.8	20.6	180	292	380
Central and South America[4]	13.7	30.1	44.7	174	399	617
Total developing	87.6	198.5	272.1	1,649	3,591	4,930
Total world	**346.7**	**500.2**	**607.7**	**5,836**	**8,146**	**10,009**

1. Includes the U.S., Canada, Mexico, Japan, France, Germany, Italy, the Netherlands, and the United Kingom. 2. China, India, and South Korea are represented in developing Asia. 3. Turkey is represented in the Middle East. 4. Brazil is represented in Central and South America.

From 1990 through 1998, the three largest producers of energy—the United States, Russia, and China—were also the three largest consumers. These three countries also make up the three top carbon dioxide emitters. Energy consumption continued to rise in both developing and industrialized nations. It is estimated that by 2020, world consumption of energy may nearly double over 1990 levels, depending on world economy (high levels of economic activity generally producing higher consumption).

32. According to the chart, is there any correlation among energy consumption, emissions, and industrialization?

(1) Industrialization correlates with emissions but not consumption.
(2) Consumption and emissions are higher among industrialized nations.
(3) Industrialization correlates with consumption but not emissions.
(4) Developing countries are high consumers and emitters.
(5) It is impossible to find any evidence for a correlation.

33. Which region can expect a leveling off of consumption from 1990–2020?

(1) Eastern Europe
(2) Asia
(3) Central and South America
(4) Middle East
(5) Africa

34. What continent might experience the sharpest increase in consumption by 2020?

(1) Europe
(2) Africa
(3) North America
(4) Antarctica
(5) Asia

35. If the world consumption of energy doubles by the year 2020, what is likely to be true about the world economy?

(1) There will be low levels of economic activity.
(2) There will be a worldwide economic recession.
(3) There will be no significant change in economic activity.
(4) There will be high levels of economic activity.
(5) The world economy will revolve around free trade.

Questions 36 through 39 refer to the following map.

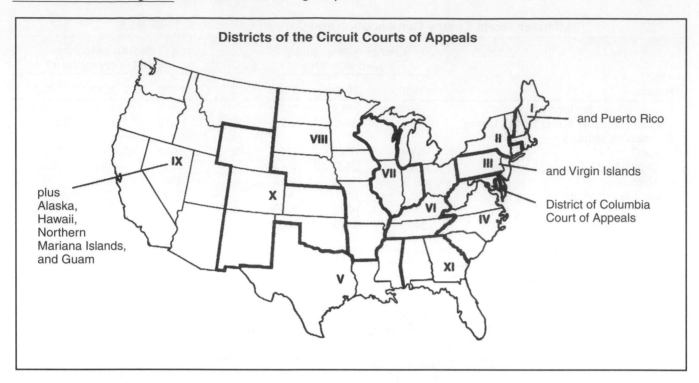

Districts of the Circuit Courts of Appeals

I ── and Puerto Rico

II

III ── and Virgin Islands

District of Columbia
Court of Appeals

plus
Alaska,
Hawaii,
Northern
Mariana Islands,
and Guam

36. According to the map, a case appealed in California would be heard by which court?

   (1) the Tenth District Court of Appeals
   (2) the Ninth District Circuit Court of Appeals
   (3) the Second District Circuit Court of Appeals
   (4) the Eighth District Circuit Court of Appeals
   (5) the Eleventh District Court of Appeals

37. Which of the following best explains why there are fewer circuit courts of appeals west of the Mississippi River?

   (1) People settle their differences on their own.
   (2) Crime is less frequent than in the area east of the Mississippi River.
   (3) There aren't many judges willing to sit on courts of appeals.
   (4) The population density is much lower than in the area east of the Mississippi River.
   (5) The courts were established much later than in the area east of the Mississippi River.

38. From looking at the map, which of the districts is made of the smallest number of states?

   (1) the Third
   (2) the Fourth
   (3) the Fifth
   (4) the Sixth
   (5) the Seventh

39. Because cases are appealed within the jurisdiction in which they were tried, what court would review an appeal registered in Chicago by a person who later moved to Indiana?

   (1) the District of Columbia Circuit Court of Appeals
   (2) the Eighth District Circuit Court of Appeals
   (3) the Seventh District Circuit Court of Appeals
   (4) the First District Circuit Court of Appeals
   (5) the Sixth District Circuit Court of Appeals

Questions 40 and 41 refer to the following graph.

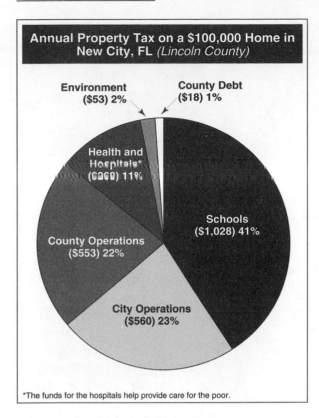

Annual Property Tax on a $100,000 Home in New City, FL (Lincoln County)

Environment ($53) 2%
County Debt ($18) 1%
Health and Hospitals* ($260) 11%
Schools ($1,028) 41%
County Operations ($553) 22%
City Operations ($560) 23%

*The funds for the hospitals help provide care for the poor.

40. Which of the following can be concluded from the graph?

(1) Lincoln County has a large unpaid debt.
(2) Lincoln County schools are expensive.
(3) The environment is a top priority for Lincoln County residents.
(4) Property taxes are high in this part of the state.
(5) Property tax monies help support both county and city government.

41. Which of the following is implied by the title of the graph?

(1) Property taxes are based on the value of the home.
(2) Property taxes are the same for every home in Lincoln County.
(3) The property tax rate never changes.
(4) Paying property taxes is voluntary.
(5) Homeowners make a one-time payment of property taxes.

42. If schooling costs an average of $10,000 annually per student, what formula below would provide full funding based on information from the graphic?

(1) State: 50%; Local 40%; Property: 10%
(2) Federal: 50%; State: 50%
(3) State: 30%; Local 40%; Property: 30%
(4) Funding is wholly the responsibility of the state.
(5) It is impossible to tell, since we have no information about the ratio of students to tax dollars.

43. Which of the following is a fact, not an opinion?

(1) Lincoln County residents have access to good health care.
(2) Property tax monies are sufficient to meet the needs of Lincoln County residents.
(3) Lincoln County must allocate more money to pay off its debt.
(4) Property tax revenues help support the schools.
(5) Education is important to help people of the state.

44. The United States Congress has joint committees which include members from both the Senate and the House of Representatives. These committees investigate and report on matters that concern both the Senate and the House. Which of the following is one of the most important jobs of a joint committee?

(1) to resolve major differences between the House and Senate over legislation
(2) to report on rules and administration
(3) to investigate the status of small businesses in the United States
(4) to investigate the reasons for the slowdown in space technology
(5) to discuss standards of official conduct

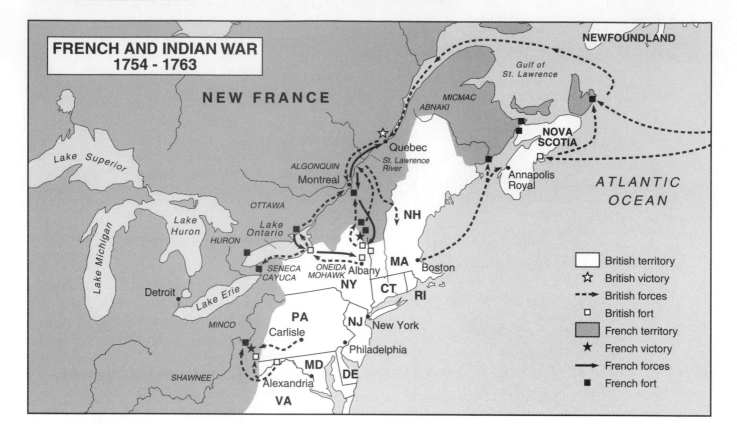

The pre-revolutionary war period contained events of great significance to U.S. history. In a rivalry carried over from European campaigns, the British and French fought over territories of colonized North America. Various Native American tribes of the Northeast allied with the French; other tribes allied with the British. Throughout the 1750s, the two sides fought over uncontrolled areas surrounding the Great Lakes. For the most part, the French held the upper hand. But in 1758, under the leadership of Britain's new prime minister, William Pitt (the elder), resources began to pour in to aid British colonies. The Royal Navy in particular maintained sea-lanes and from 1759 through 1763, Britain won successive battles, forcing the French forces north and producing the Treaty of Paris in February 1763. Britain's support came with a price tag, however. Its financial resources depleted, the British government instituted a series of taxes on the colonies—taxes that would later culminate in a new battle cry: "No taxation without representation!"

45. Which of the following is supported by the map and passage?

(1) There is no relation between the Great Lakes and battles in the war.
(2) It is impossible to discern a relation from the map.
(3) The map tells us that all battles were fought on the Great Lakes.
(4) The passage tells us that all battles were probably fought along the Great Lakes.
(5) The map and the passage suggest that the Great Lakes facilitated transportation.

46. Which of the following can be concluded from the map and the passage?

    (1) The French were hampered by inadequate naval support.
    (2) The French fought bravely.
    (3) Native American Indian tribes fought exclusively for the French.
    (4) The British drove the French from North America.
    (5) The British had better generals than the French.

47. According to the map, which of the following is true about the eventual boundary between the United States and Canada?

    (1) The map does not provide information about the boundary.
    (2) The boundary was drawn along the St. Lawrence River.
    (3) The boundary now runs along the Hudson River.
    (4) The boundary was established along previously British and French territories.
    (5) The boundary was established before the French and Indian War.

48. Which of the following best explains how the French and Indian War later affected U.S. history?

    (1) It established final borderlines between Canada and the U.S.
    (2) It strengthened ties between Europeans and American Native Indians.
    (3) It led to friction between the colonists and Britain.
    (4) It left the American colonists open to invasion by the French.
    (5) It helped establish trade routes to the Northwest.

Question 49 refers to the following cartoon.

Arthur A. Henrikson. The Daily Herald.

49. Which of the following statements best summarizes the cartoonist's attitude toward mergers?

    (1) They always happen fast.
    (2) They are bad for consumers.
    (3) Elevator companies should not merge.
    (4) Consumers should beware before buying stock.
    (5) Only lawyers should investigate mergers.

50. Economic inflation is an overall and often disproportionate increase in price levels. Inflation of the dollar means that a consumer can buy less with a set amount of money than was possible earlier. When inflation continues to develop, which of the following best explains what happens?

    (1) The consumer's budget is stretched to its limit.
    (2) The size of the dollar bill gets larger.
    (3) The bill collector's voice gets louder.
    (4) The cost of living goes up.
    (5) A consumer often has to get a second job to keep up with the bills.

SOCIAL STUDIES

The chart below will help you determine your strengths and weaknesses on the content and skill areas of the GED Social Studies Test. Use the Answers and Explanations starting on page 106 to check your answers on the test.

Directions: Circle the number of each item that you answered correctly on the Simulated GED Test B. Count the number of items you answered correctly in each column. Write the amount in the Total Correct space of each column. (For example, if you answered 8 U.S. History items correctly, place the number 8 in the blank before out of 12.) Complete this process for the remaining columns.

Count the number of items you answered correctly in each row. Write that amount in the Total Correct space of each row. (For example, in the Comprehension row, write the number correct in the blank before out of 10.) Complete this process for the remaining rows.

Content / Cognitive Level	United States History (Unit 1)	World History (Unit 2)	Civic and Government (Unit 3)	Economics (Unit 4)	Geography (Unit 5)	Total Correct
Comprehension		7*, 9*	18*, 36, 40, 41	11, 49	33*	_____ out of 9
Application	10*, 23, 25, 27		17*, 39, 44	15, 26, 31	34*	_____ out of 11
Analysis	2, 21*, 30, 48*	1, 5*, 6*, 24	16*, 19*, 37, 38, 42, 43	12, 13, 29	3, 4, 35*	_____ out of 20
Evaluation	20*, 28, 46*, 47*	8*, 22		14, 50	32*, 45*	_____ out of 10
Total Correct	_____ out of 12	_____ out of 8	_____ out of 13	_____ out of 9	_____ out of 7	Total Correct: _____ out of 50 1–40 = You need more review. 41–50 = Congratulations! You're ready.

Boldface items indicate questions that include graphics.
Boldface items with an asterisk (*) indicate questions with a combination of a graphic and a prose passage.

If you answered fewer than 41 questions correctly, determine which areas are hardest for you. Go back to the *Steck-Vaughn GED Social Studies* book and review the content in those specific areas.

In the parentheses beneath the heading, the units tell you where you can find specific instruction about that area in the *Steck-Vaughn GED Social Studies* book. Also refer to the chart on page 3 of this book.

UNIT 1: United States History

Pages 4–15

1. **(3) Italians were skilled navigators.** (Evaluation) All the explorers listed were Italian. Option (1) is wrong because Columbus was looking for India, not a new continent. There is no evidence in the passage for options (2) or (4). Option (5) is true, but the passage only suggests that the Atlantic Ocean lies between Europe and the Americas.

2. **(2) Because Italy was not a strong unified country, its explorers had to turn to other countries for financial support.** (Evaluation) There was a relatively large number of Italian explorers, yet they all were in the service of other countries and Italy is not listed among the countries that colonized the Americas. There is no support in the passage for options (1), (3), (4), and (5).

3. **(1) the later colonization patterns** (Analysis) The British colonized parts of the Eastern seaboard, and the Spanish colonized the South American region. There is no support for the other options in the passage.

4. **(2) Neither explorer had really reached the mainland.** (Analysis) Both Cabot and Columbus reached only outlying islands of the lands. Options (1) and (4) would have no influence on what the Americas were called. Option (3) does not explain why Spain didn't choose its first explorer. Option (5) is false.

5. **(3) making money** (Evaluation) Only profit-making is explicitly mentioned in the passage. The remaining options are either factually wrong (1) or unsupported by the evidence. Political independence and democracy were not yet issues.

6. **(2) They could not otherwise afford to make a new life in the Americas.** (Analysis) Option (2) provides a sound economic reason. There is no support for option (1) in the passage; being in debtor's prison is not the same as being a fugitive. There is no evidence in the passage for options (3) and (5). Option (4) may have been true for some people but does not explain why they went to America.

7. **(2) by grants of land subject to the English Crown** (Comprehension) Because the land was claimed by the country, settlement could occur only with government approval. Options (1) and (3) have no support in the passage. Option (4) is true but has nothing to do with systematic colonization. Option (5) was not quite true.

8. **(2) People have the right to privacy of property.** (Comprehension) Locke believed the government should not interfere with private property. There is no support for options (1) or (5). Options (3) and (4) are contradicted by the passage.

9. **(1) colonists who objected to having to house British troops** (Application) Locke would support the colonists' objection to an invasion of their private property. Options (2), (3), and (5) are not relevant to the violation of citizens' rights. Locke would not have supported option (4).

10. **(2) No taxation without representation.** (Application) Proper representation was one of Locke's points. Although the other options are phrases associated with the American Revolution, they do not reflect the philosopher's beliefs.

11. **(1) The argument attacks the person rather than the issue of a violation of rights.** (Evaluation) Locke would be most concerned with the issue. Option (3) is a logical fallacy. There is no support for options (2), (4), and (5) in the passage.

12. **(4) It had greater resources and labor forces than the South.** (Comprehension) Only statistics for option (4) are given. Statistics for options (1), (2), and (3) are not given. There is no support for option (5) in the graph.

13. **(1) It was through sheer determination on the part of the South that the war lasted four years.** (Evaluation) This is a comment on what people can do with very few resources. There is no evidence for options (2), (3), and (5). Option (4) is wrong because it is false and lacks evidence.

14. **(3) The South had to spend money it desperately needed buying manufactured products from Europe.** (Analysis) The graph shows that the South had far fewer bank assets or manufactured goods than the North. Therefore, bank assets, which were much needed, had to go for manufactured goods (previously supplied by the North). Options (1), (2), and (5), while problems for the South, are unrelated to any information in the graph. Option (4) would have made the population gap between North and South worse, but was not the cause of it.

15. **(3) a major American tragedy** (Application) The casualties of the Civil War were staggering. The death tolls have nothing to do with options (1), (2) or (4). Option (5) is unclear.

16. **(2) friends and relatives were often among the enemy dead** (Application) There is no evidence for options (1) and (3) on the graph. Options (4) and (5) would have no bearing on the effect of the losses.

17. **(1) a serious shortage of workers** (Analysis) The large number of lives lost would have an adverse effect on the labor force but would not result in the other options.

18. **(5) Northern victory in the Civil War ensured the emergence of the United States as a world power.** (Analysis) The United States didn't emerge as a world power until decades later. Many events and factors could have influenced the emergence of the United States as a world power. Furthermore, there is no way of knowing what would have happened had the North not won the Civil War. For these reasons, the statement is an opinion rather than a fact. Options (1), (2), (3), and (4) are all facts.

19. **(4) to discourage the secession of states** (Analysis) Only this option is supported by the references to the perpetuity of the Union. The remaining options are either factually wrong (the Civil War had not begun) or unsupported.

20. **(5) development of agricultural cooperatives to handle and sell products** (Comprehension) There is nothing in the passage about farmers coming together to form agricultural cooperatives. Options (1), (3), and (4) are mentioned in the passage. Option (2) is implied by the increased farm size and by the movement of farmers to cities.

21. **(3) The Industrial Revolution probably changed a large number of lifestyles in America.** (Comprehension) Although only craftspeople and farmers are discussed in this passage, there is an implication that other occupations were affected. Options (1) and (2) contradict the information given. Options (4) and (5) have no support in the passage.

22. **(4) They were looking for jobs.** (Analysis) Options (1) and (2) have no support in the passage. Although options (3) and (5) might be true, neither was discussed or implied in the passage.

23. **(5) All self-sufficient farmers had to become cash-crop farmers.** (Comprehension) There is no evidence that all farmers turned to cash crops. Options (1), (2), (3), and (4) are not supported by the information in the passage.

24. **(3) computer technology** (Application) Computer technology has changed many facets of everyday life because it has required retraining or relocation for employment and has made a number of products available to people who previously could not afford them. Options (1), (2), (4), and (5) have not affected as many people as option (3).

25. **(3) Within one century, the American economy shifted from being primarily agrarian to a more industrial economy.** (Evaluation) An agrarian economy requires a large rural population, and an industrial economy requires a large urban population. Although option (1) is true, no figures are given for the origins of the growing urban population. There is no evidence on the graph for option (2). Options (4) and (5) are incorrect according to the graph.

26. **(2) They manufactured votes.** (Application) Machines are used to manufacture items in the same way that political machines produced the desired number of votes by buying them. The other options may be true, but they do not suggest a mechanical process.

27. **(2) the growing number of services that cities had to provide** (Analysis) Traditional governments were inadequate to meet the needs of greatly increased populations. Political machines stepped in to fill these needs. There is no support in the passage for options (1), (3), and (4). Option (5) is contradicted by the passage, which indicates that power in cities was divided.

28. **(3) The businesses could pay corrupt politicians to leave them alone.** (Analysis) Political machines were interested in money and power, and they would turn a blind eye if the price was right. There is not enough evidence for options (1), (2), or (4) in the passage. Option (5) is unlikely because the political machines were too powerful.

29. **(3) the land could no longer support its weight** (Analysis) The weight of skyscrapers combined with the removal of the natural support of earth in building subways is suggested as the cause of collapse. Option (1) might apply to San Francisco but is not supported in the cartoon. Options (2) and (5) are not suggested in the cartoon. Option (4) may be the reason for the building of skyscrapers, but it is not the direct cause for the sinking of the city.

30. **(1) growth of a city is not always good** (Analysis) City growth is usually considered to be progress, but in the cartoon it is interpreted as a destructive force. Options (2) and (3) refer to minor elements of the cartoon, not to the opinion they convey. Option (4) is too general. There is no evidence in the cartoon for option (5).

31. (1) Too Much a Sign of the Times
(Application) The main idea of the cartoon is that there are too many outdoor advertising signs cluttering the cityscape solely in the interest of making money. There is no support for options (2) and (3) in the cartoon. Option (4) is wrong because the implication is that the signs are not really art. Option (5) may be an indirect cause of the use of signs, but it is not the focus of the cartoon.

32. (3) the money involved in advertising
(Comprehension) The dollar sign on the bag indicates money. The fact that it is tied to both buildings and signs represents that it is related to advertising. Option (2) ignores the cartoon's main concern. There is no evidence for options (1), (4), and (5) in the cartoon.

33. (1) a blight on the urban landscape
(Comprehension) The city is overrun with ugly and misleading (option 3) advertising, the opposite of art (option 4), as represented by the woman (option 2).

34. (1) in the phrase "Rosie the riveter"
(Application) The phrase captures the idea of a woman working in a tough job that is especially important to the war effort. Options (2) and (4) are incorrect because they emphasize the domestic role of women. Option (3) is not a reflection of the importance of these women. Option (5) is wrong because Carry Nation was a temperance crusader in the 1800s.

35. (3) Women had already proved that they could do the jobs. (Analysis) The women realized that equal work deserved equal pay. There is no evidence for options (1) and (2) in the passage. Options (4) and (5) do not explain the working women's dissatisfaction.

36. (2) Women have participated in the civilian labor force in increasing numbers. (Analysis) Only this option is supported by the numbers. There is no information or support for Option (4). The remaining options are factually incorrect.

37. (4) a student with poor math skills
(Comprehension) The boy wearing dark glasses does not know the simple fact that a half dozen is six; this eliminates option (5). There is not enough evidence in the cartoon for option (1). There is no support in the cartoon for option (2). Wearing headphones is not sufficient to suggest option (3).

38. (1) not simply isolated names and dates
(Analysis) Historical events affect culture and social activity, and are, therefore, more than dry facts. There is no support in this passage for options (2) and (5). Option (3) may be true occasionally but not always. Option (4) is logically incorrect; the events in themselves are not symbols.

39. (3) a reaffirmation of some American ideals (Application) Much of the music dealt in some way with the concepts of life, liberty, and the pursuit of happiness. Options (1) and (2) are contradicted by evidence in the passage. There is no support for options (4) and (5) in the passage.

40. (1) influenced the values of American youth (Application) Political values can be shaped by a cultural medium. Although some people might like to believe options (2), (3), and (4), none are true. Option (5) is wrong because this period was not one of innocence.

41. (2) politically aware (Evaluation) Most of the discussion concerns reactions to political situations. There is no evidence for options (1) and (3) in the passage. Option (4) is eliminated by the reference to the patriotic song by Sadler. Dylan's songs of social protest eliminate option (5).

42. (1) decrease U.S. defense budgets (Analysis) Since Soviet expansion, which the U.S. would prevent by military means, was no longer a possibility, U.S. military spending could be reduced. Option (2) is contradicted by the passage, since as the remaining superpower, the U.S. would be likely to have even more influence. There is no support for options (3) and (4). Option (5) is unlikely, as one of the U.S.'s major international concerns no longer existed.

43. (2) from many points of view
(Comprehension) Several views of history are mentioned. The other options are not supported by the passage.

44. (4) It repeats itself. (Analysis) The implication is that people either did not pay attention to or did not learn from past events and made the same mistakes. Options (1), (3), and (5) are true but are not related to the suggestion. Option (2) is true only in some cases and is not a result of the suggestion.

45. (3) Current events eventually become part of the historical record. (Comprehension) The phrase suggests that today's newsworthy events will be less newsworthy tomorrow. The other options are not true.

46. (2) history being rewritten (Application)
With additional information, the historical
view of this event will have changed, and the
record of it will have been revised. Options (1),
(3), and (4) are not concerned with the new
perspective. Option (5) is wrong because it
assumes no further information can be
discovered.

**47. (5) The past affects the lives of people in
the present.** (Evaluation) It is suggested that
understanding how the past affects the present
will give insight into how to plan for the future.
Although options (1), (2), (3), and (4) are often
true, they are only aspects of the recording and
understanding of the historical process.

**48. (1) Lincoln won a decisive electoral
victory.** (Evaluation) Only this option is
supported by the evidence. None of the other
options can be inferred.

**49. (3) production of electricity for the
Tennessee Valley** (Analysis) Only option (3)
does not limit the freedom of choice for either
the individual or the state. All the other options
are examples of government restrictions and
intervention.

**50. (3) Capitalism has some problems, which
the government should try to deal with
through regulation.** (Analysis) Economic
troubles were an indication that capitalism had
problems. The New Deal legislation and
agencies were an attempt to regulate capitalism.
Therefore, options (2), (4), and (5) are incorrect.
But the New Deal did not seek government
control over businesses, so option (1) is
incorrect.

51. (1) save human and natural resources
(Comprehension) This option summarizes the
intent of the majority of New Deal programs.
Option (2) has no support in the passage.
Options (3), (4), and (5) are wrong because they
are all only aspects of option (1).

**52. (2) The programs were known by many
initials.** (Comprehension) The jumble of
initials gives the impression of alphabet soup.
There is no support for options (1), (3), and (4)
in the passage. Option (5) is probably true, but
it is not a reason for the nickname.

**53. (4) Millions of workers were paid by the
government.** (Evaluation) Government
funding means government spending. None of
the other options are related to the financial
situation of the government itself.

**54. (2) Grover Cleveland, like Al Gore, won
the popular vote but lost in the Electoral
College** (Analysis) Only this option is
supported by the passage. Options (1) and (5)
are contradicted by Article II. Options (3) and
(4) cannot be inferred.

55. (5) Alaska (Analysis) Each state's electors
include the senators (2) and as many
representatives as the state possesses. Only
Alaska of the states mentioned has a total of
three electors.

**56. (1) It has declined as a percentage since
1960.** (Evaluation) This option is supported by
the chart. The remaining options are either
factually untrue, or, in the case of option (4)
impossible to infer.

UNIT 2: World History

Pages 16–23

**1. (2) Phoenician traders transmitted their
alphabet throughout the Mediterranean.**
(Analysis) As traders, the Phoenicians
transmitted goods and used their alphabet to
transmit their culture. Options (1) and (3)
cannot be inferred from the passage and are
dubious at best. Options (4) and (5) are
contradicted by the passage.

**2. (1) It is the largest religious complex
ever created.** (Comprehension) According to
the text, Angkor is the largest collection of
religious structures ever created. Options (3),
(4), and (5) are not supported by the text.
Nothing in the text suggests that the sack of
Angkor was synonymous with option (2).

3. (2) irrigation (Application) Option (2) is the
only suitable use for the huge water repositories
and systems mentioned. Options (1), (3), and
(4), while possible, are more recreational and
less important. Option (5) was not an activity
available in the time period mentioned.

4. (3) to demonstrate imperial power
(Analysis) Although the fortifications were
probably intended as defensive, nothing in the
passage suggests fear of an Indian incursion.
Instead, the competitiveness of successive kings
to build the biggest edifice suggests attempts to
display power. Options (2), (4), and (5) cannot
be inferred.

5. (2) increased competition (Comprehension)
The passage states that the North West
Company "galvanized" Hudson Bay into
action. Option (1) is illogical. Option (3) is
contradicted by the information. Options (4)
and (5) are unsupported.

6. **(3) facilitate transportation of fur** (Analysis). The location of a settlement where two trade routes join suggests that transportation is a factor. Options (1), (2), and (4) are either unsupported or unlikely. Option (5) has no basis of support in the passage and cannot be inferred.

7. **(4) The fur trade reached across territorial limits.** (Evaluation) The passage and map support this conclusion (witness the trade routes throughout the western reaches of Canada and the U.S.) Option (1) is a value judgment, not a conclusion. The remaining options may or may not be true, but are not supported by the evidence.

8. **(2) the stars** (Comprehension) The celestial reckoning mentioned in the passage refers to stars. The remaining options are either unsupported or contradicted by the evidence.

9. **(4) chronometer** (Application) The chronometer, Option (4), was the key instrument in accurate determination of longitude, which permitted the creation of international time zones. Options (1) and (2), while important instruments, were not the critical inventions in this case. Options (3) and (5) are not relevant to the establishment of time zones.

10. **(3) Time zones regularized schedules across local and national lines.** (Analysis) This answer implies two assumptions: that formal time zones regularized times within each zone and that trains work in conjunction with each other. Option (1) supposes the need to understand absolute solar time. Options (2) and (5) are illogical. Option (4) is not relevant.

11. **(1) the location of the Royal Greenwich Observatory near London** (Application) The map rules out options (2), (4), and (5). Option (3) is irrelevant. Option (1) is also implied by the centrality of British know-how in the "discovery" of longitude.

12. **(2) It slowed industrialization by tying former serfs to rural lives.** (Analysis) Option (2) can be arrived at by eliminating the remaining options. Option (1) cannot be supported. Option (3) is illogical, as the passage states that serfs were charged for land. Options (4) and (5) are illogical in that these actions would discourage industrialization.

13. **(1) industrial countries** (Comprehension) This option is the only one in the passage. The other options, which may all be serviced by railroads, are not mentioned in the text.

14. **(2) Railroad travel was declining at the end of the twentieth century.** (Application) Only option (2) accurately reflects the statistics presented in the passage. Option (1) is contradicted by the text. Options (3), (4), and (5) are not mentioned and cannot be concluded from the text.

15. **(4) dominated by foreign interests** (Analysis) Only this option can be concluded from the table. The influence of foreign interests—British, French, and Japanese—is felt to be dominating by the Chinese, thus the resistance. Options (1), (2) and (3) are contradicted by the evidence. Option (5) is contrary to unstated assumptions about rebellions and resistance.

16. **(3) a comparison of total soldiers killed on both sides to total civilians dead** (Evaluation) Only this option adequately isolates the factors assumed by the question. Options (1) and (5) are irrelevant; option (2) is misleading; option (4) provides inadequate information.

17. **(4) Portugal** (Comprehension) A comparison of figures shows that Portugal lost its entire military force.

18. **(2) Greece** (Comprehension) According to the tables, Greece is the only country of those listed that lost more civilians than soldiers.

19. **(2) machine guns** (Analysis) Only machine guns would have inflicted massive ground casualties. The remaining options either were not available during World War I or did not contribute to casualties (option 3).

20. **(4) Germany** (Comprehension) A comparison of total dollars yields this conclusion. The remaining options are ruled out.

21. **(4) Britain and France annexed the majority of African territory.** (Evaluation) The map indicates that France and Britain established the most and largest colonial territories in Africa. Options (1), (3), and (5) are incorrect. Option (2) may be true, but it is not supported by the map.

22. **(4) inefficiency in colonial matters** (Analysis) Option (4) is the only one pertinent to the information given. The other options are outside the scope of the information or do not bear directly on Portugal's decline in Africa.

23. **(1) Belgium** (Comprehension) The map shows that the only Belgian colony is completely landlocked. All the other options are countries whose colonies have access to the sea.

24. **(1) Colonialism waned in the twentieth century** (Analysis) Only this statement is a conclusion supported by the evidence. The remaining options are either contradicted (2), unsupported (3) and (5), or constitute an opinion (4).

25. **(1) neutrality in the Cold War** (Analysis) Nehru is attempting to state his case, both to the U.S. and to the world. This answer requires recognizing historical context and understanding the effort to persuade. Options (2) and (5) may be implied, but are not central to the historical context nor to the speech's purpose. Options (3) and (4) are irrelevant.

26. **(2) student exchanges** (Analysis) Based on Nehru's speech, only option (2) is supported. The other options directly contradict his beliefs about nonaggression and non-interference in the affairs of other countries.

27. **(4) Nehru would be willing to open trade negotiations with the Soviet Union.** (Analysis) Option (4) is a valid conclusion from the passage that free trade and friendly relations with other countries were goals of the Prime Minister. The other options run counter to the policies stated in the speech.

28. **(3) independence from Britain** (Analysis) Of all the options, this not only fits with Indian history, but also explains the connotations of "freedom." The remaining options are either irrelevant or unsupported.

29. **(2) He wanted to justify India's position of nonalignment to the U.S.** (Analysis) Option 2 summarizes the main point of Nehru's statement. None of the other options is supported by the information in the passage.

30. **(2) It must be protected.** (Analysis) The delicacy of the plant and its need for protection are the salient aspects of the cartoon. Options (1) and (3) are either unsupported or contrary to the cartoon's spirit. Options (4) and (5) are either too literal or illogical.

31. **(1) differences among ethnic groups** (Analysis) The passage refers to homogeneous states, contrasting with Bosnia. Options (2) and (4) are irrelevant. Option (3) is an unlikely cause. Option (5) is unsupported.

32. **(2) opposition to democracy** (Evaluation) From the protesters' point of view, the tank represents oppression. Thus, options (1), (4), and (5) are ruled out. Option (3) is less likely than option (2) given the fact that the man is clearly protesting in opposition to the nation.

UNIT 3: Civics and Government

Pages 24–34

1. **(1) Dependency on others makes people dependent on government.** (Comprehension) Since consumers depend on producers whose primary motive is profit, consumers must depend on government to ensure public safety and health. Options (2) and (5) are the opposite of what is stated in the passage. Option (3) is implied in the passage but does not represent the main idea. Option (4) is not supported by the passage.

2. **(1) by passing laws** (Application) Laws set limits on behavior and help to prevent infringement on rights. Options (2), (3), and (5) have no legal effect. Option (4) may lead to a law but does not ensure anything.

3. **(5) to impose economic order on society** (Analysis) A government structure can regulate the exchange of goods and services. Options (1), (3), and (4) are not supported by the passage. Option (2) is not a primary government concern.

4. **(1) The Senate has been under Republican rule for most of the last two decades.** (Evaluation) This conclusion is supported by the numbers in the chart. The answer is also evident through a process of elimination: none of the other options are supported by the evidence.

5. **(2) All people should be given the same respect.** (Comprehension) Equality is used in a general sense of all individuals being human and having the same rights. Options (1), (3), and (5) are wrong because equal does not mean identical. Option (4) is a denial of basic rights.

6. **(3) a set of beliefs** (Evaluation) None of the principles can be proved; thus option (1) is eliminated. Options (4) and (5) are also based on belief and not fact. Option (2) is not suggested in the text.

7. **(4) question the validity of a law** (Application) A law can be questioned because there is no absolute truth, and people have the right to make choices. Options (1), (2), (3), and (5) violate the rights of others.

8. **(2) encourage a friend to vote even though the friend favors another candidate** (Application) The person would encourage the friend to vote, because every individual is entitled to freedom of choice. Option (1) contradicts democratic principles because it would make it difficult for a person with little personal wealth to run for office. Options (3) and (5) contradict the principles that all individuals are equal and that every individual has value. Option (4) contradicts the principle that there is no absolute truth because it would not allow new voices in government.

9. **(3) They don't seem to be able to speak for themselves.** (Comprehension) The labels on the briefcases refer to elements in a speech that should not have to be provided for the speaker. Option (1) is not an opinion. Options (2), (4), and (5) may be true but are not suggested in this cartoon.

10. **(3) The news media often publicize the details of a crime before it comes to trial.** (Analysis) When the Sixth Amendment was written, there were no TVs or radios or even news reporters. Today the public can form an opinion even before a case is tried. There is no support for the other options; none of them would affect impartiality.

11. **(5) A Fair Trial** (Application) The Sixth Amendment was written to prevent unfair treatment of the accused. Options (1), (2), and (3) are not addressed by the amendment. Option (4) is incorrect because only aspects of the process are mentioned.

12. **(3) unjust imprisonment** (Evaluation) Only if the accused is able to present a defense can unjust imprisonment be avoided. Options (1) and (2) cannot be prevented by law. There is no evidence for options (4) and (5) in the passage.

13. **(4) ensure that working Americans benefit from economic growth** (Comprehension) President Clinton said, "...those who work and lift this nation must have more of its benefits." Options (1) and (3) are incorrect because President Clinton referred to income growth, not jobs for middle-class Americans. Options (2) and (5) are not supported by the excerpt.

14. **(5) reward workers who come up with cost-saving ideas** (Application) This proposal would protect workers' jobs and reward workers for their contributions, both of which Clinton favored. Therefore, options (1), (2), and (3) are incorrect. Option (4) is not supported by the excerpt.

15. **(3) Opinion polls are mistakenly regarded as important.** (Analysis) The cartoonist is suggesting that some people regard response to a poll as equal to voting even though polls have no effect on the outcome of an election. Options (1), (2), and (5) are wrong because only a vote affects the political process. There is no evidence for option (4) in the cartoon.

16. **(1) Some Americans do not really understand the political process.** (Analysis) Confusion about the importance of an opinion poll indicates a misunderstanding of the political process. The cartoonist may believe option (4), but in this cartoon the focus is on the attitude of the public and not the worth of a poll. Option (3) is false. There is insufficient evidence in the cartoon for options (2) and (5), but they are also unlikely considering the nature of the cartoon.

17. **(3) Not all voters are satisfied with the two major parties.** (Analysis) A third party on a ballot means that enough people were not happy with the other choices. Options (1) and (5) are wrong because the inclusion is evidence of change instead of decay. There is not enough support for options (2) and (4) in the text.

18. **(2) a pressure group at work** (Application) The company is trying to persuade through pressure, a common and legal practice. Therefore, options (1) and (5) are wrong. There is no support for option (3) in the text. Option (4) is wrong because it does not refer to the group's action.

19. **(2) Voting will give you a voice in how government is run.** (Evaluation) By voting, citizens can express their ideas about government policies and elect representatives who will act on the voters' behalf. Options (1), (3), (4), and (5) are not supported by the passage.

20. **(3) It goes against democratic principles.** (Evaluation) The passage states that democracy is based upon the right to vote and that voting is a way for the average person to exercise power. Option (1) is incorrect, because often, a higher voter turnout can bring about political change. Options (2), (4), and (5) are contradicted by the passage.

21. **(2) Power is centered on an individual who could fail or die.** (Analysis) Although all the other options are often true, what makes the government unstable is that it is held together because of the personality of one person. When that person is no longer in charge, the basis for rule disappears.

22. **(4) a monarchy** (Application) Leadership in a monarchy is usually attained by inheritance or through marriage to a member of the royal family. Leadership in the other options is achieved through election, appointment, or by overthrowing the previous government.

23. **(1) the office itself** (Evaluation) The obligations of the officials are defined by laws. Options (2) and (3) are eliminated by option (1). Options (4) and (5) are not suggested or supported by the definitions.

24. **(2) "Less government regulation will help the economy."** (Application) Because conservatives believe that the health of the economy is tied to the health of industry, they would likely oppose regulatory policies that could affect corporate profits. Options (1) and (3) are not supported by the passage. Option (4) is incorrect because most conservatives favor lowering taxes. Option (5) is incorrect because it represents a liberal point of view as described in the passage.

25. **(3) Conservatives and liberals differ in their ideas about the role of government.** (Evaluation) Conservatives believe that government should play less of a role in Americans' lives, whereas liberals believe that government should play a key role in addressing economic and social issues. Options (1), (2), and (4) are incorrect because they contradict information in the passage. Option (5) is not supported by the passage.

26. **(5) economic issues** (Analysis) The passage compares how conservatives and liberals approach issues such as taxes, the federal deficit, and social welfare programs. Options (1), (2), (3), and (4) are not supported by the passage.

27. **(4) permits the President to delegate some duties to aides** (Comprehension) The law concerns people the President can designate to act for him or her. The law does not limit the President's responsibilities as suggested in option (1) or add to the duties of the President as suggested by option (2). The President is still responsible for all who act for him, so option (3) is wrong. The law relieves the President of some duties but not all of them as stated in option (5).

28. **(4) Superman** (Application) Wilson implies that only extraordinary people could handle the demands of the presidency if the task isn't lightened a bit. Candidates would have to be exceptionally intelligent and strong. Options (1), (2), and (3) are characters who break under the strain. Option (5) only has strength.

`29. **(2) An understanding of a part helps in understanding the whole.** (Application) The President must be familiar with all aspects of the job and with the details in order to make the major decisions. Options (1) and (4) contradict this idea. Option (3) is wrong because some balance is needed. There is no support for option (5) in the passage.

30. **(1) many and complex** (Evaluation) Some of the duties listed in the passage cover a wide range of abilities. The suggestion that an ordinary person would break under the stress of the office eliminates options (2) and (4). There is no support in the passage for option (3) except for minor functions. Option (5) may be true of some duties, but some also appear fairly ordinary.

31. **(1) barring cigarette ads in publications that reach minors** (Application) This is the only option that relates to free speech; therefore, the other options are incorrect.

32. **(5) desegregation in public schools** (Analysis) The Supreme Court decision disputed the premise of segregation, that blacks and whites taught in separate educational facilities could still receive equal education. Options (1), (3), and (4) are not supported by the passage. Option (2) is incorrect because it is opposite of what the passage implies—that the court's purpose was to create greater equality in education.

33. **(1) three** (Comprehension) Pennsylvania, Maryland, and North Carolina split their votes. The other options are incorrect.

34. **(3) It was a strategy to guarantee Adams as President if the Federalist party had a majority.** (Analysis) By casting a vote for Jay, Federalists made sure Adams had one more vote than Pinckney. There is insufficient evidence for the other options. Option (4) is incorrect because there is no evidence of who voted for Jay.

35. **(5) Indiana didn't have a vote because it wasn't a state.** (Evaluation) Indiana is clearly marked as a territory; only states voted. There is no support for option (1) by the facts on the map. Option (2) is wrong because New England was solidly behind Adams. Options (3) and (4) are wrong because there is no information about the popular vote on the map.

36. **(3) who actually became President** (Evaluation) Because Jefferson and Burr received the same number of votes, either one could become President. The map does not have the information of who did become President. All of the other options are on the map.

37. **(2) an unsigned bill that comes to the President just before a congressional adjournment** (Analysis) According to the passage, the only alternative to a veto (where the President sends the bill back with objections) occurs when the Congress adjourns. Options (1) and (5) are unlikely. Options (3) and (4) are not supported by the passage.

38. **(1) Vetoes were used more frequently in the twentieth century than in the nineteenth century.** (Analysis) The answer requires inferring from knowledge of presidential dates. Options (2), (3), and (5) are not supported by the evidence. Option (4) cannot be inferred.

39. **(1) Bush carried the southern states.** (Analysis) The answer can be derived from observation of the map and elimination of the alternative options, which are not supported by the evidence.

40. **(3) The electoral college, not the majority of voters in the country, elects the President.** (Analysis) This answer can be inferred from evidence from the passage and the map. Options (1), (2) and (4) are contradicted by either the passage or the map. Option (5) is contradicted by common sense.

41. **(2) It stopped a recount.** (Analysis) This answer can be inferred from the passage, which summarizes the Supreme Court ruling. Options (1) and (4) are unlikely. Option (3) is contradicted by the evidence. Option (5) may be true, but is irrelevant.

42. **(1) stopping domestic terrorism is a top priority** (Comprehension) The massive government response suggests this answer. There is no support for options (2), (3), or (4). Option (5) is incorrect because the passage addresses domestic terrorism, not international terrorism.

43. **(2) Senior citizens have political clout.** (Comprehension) Because the elderly represent a large percentage of the voting population, lawmakers are reluctant to cut programs seniors support. Options (1), (3), and (5) are not addressed in the passage. Option (4) is the opposite of what the passage implies.

44. **(3) People without health insurance can't afford care.** (Analysis) According to the passage, Americans are concerned because the high cost of medical care limits access to care for the uninsured. Options (1), (2), and (4) are supporting statements, not conclusions. Option (5) is not supported by the passage.

45. **(1) relieved some workers of unwanted political connections** (Analysis) Joining a union would have meant accepting that union's political position. Options (2) and (3) imply a faulty cause and effect. Option (4) has no support in the passage. Option (5) is wrong because having fewer members would not end the unions; it would only weaken them.

46. **(4) a low property tax rate** (Application) Offering a low property tax rate would be an incentive to a business. Option (3) would drive a business away. Options (1), (2), and (5) are incorrect because a city cannot change state or federal tax rates.

47. **(2) Keeping voters and campaign contributors happy helps lawmakers get reelected.** (Analysis) Option (1), (3), and (4) are not supported by the passage. Option (5) does not explain why it is difficult to stop the practice.

48. **(4) Bringing Home the Bacon** (Application) "Pork" often refers to funding for special projects in Congressional members' home districts. Option (1) is incorrect because it denotes consumption rather than practices that further political self interest. Option (2) is incorrect because it implies corruption, and pork-barrel politics is legal. Option (3) is unlikely because it implies contentment, not rewards for political favors. Option (5) is incorrect because it refers to a lifestyle.

49. **(3) legislation that reflects a conservative agenda** (Evaluation) Option (1) is incorrect because the passage focuses on political change rather than conflict. Options (2) and (4) are unlikely. There would probably be more change and more vetoes. There is no support for option (5).

UNIT 4: Economics

Pages 35–44

1. **(4) spends more than it earns** (Application) The U.S. imported more than it exported; that is, it spent more money buying foreign goods than it earned selling U.S. goods. Options (1), (2), and (5) are not supported by the passage. Option (3) is contradicted, since the U.S., spending more than it earned, could not have saved money.

2. **(2) U.S. consumers buying fewer Pacific Rim cars and electronics** (Analysis) The U.S. has a large trade deficit with the countries of the Pacific Rim. So fewer purchases would have the greatest effect on the overall balance of trade. Option (1) would affect the overall trade gap, but only minutely. Options (3), (4), and (5) are incorrect or unsupported by the evidence.

3. **(2) The instruments of economics are inaccurate.** (Comprehension) Options (1) and (3) are wrong because they are based on a misreading of the text. Option (4) is wrong because some solutions are found. Option (5) does not answer the question. Evidence for the correct option is in the second paragraph.

4. **(5) knowing how to balance the national budget without additional taxation** (Application) Balancing the national budget without additional taxation is the only complex economic problem not mentioned in the passage. Options (1) and (4) are not complex problems of economics. Options (2) and (3) are wrong because they are examples already provided by the author.

5. **(2) Economists can prevent economic depressions.** (Analysis) The author believes that economists have the tools to avoid depressions, but this has not been proven. The other options are facts.

6. **(4) It's based on more than just financial data.** (Evaluation) Economic study relies on data from the other social sciences. The passage does not support options (1) and (3) and contradicts option (2). Option (5) is an incorrect conclusion.

7. **(2) It's a serious problem.** (Comprehension) The deficit is a serious drain on federal resources. It is not a joke as suggested by option (1), nor is it easily resolved as suggested by option (5). Neither option (3) nor option (4) is suggested in the cartoon.

8. **(3) reckless gambling** (Analysis) Throwing good money after bad is a waste and a thoughtless gamble. The other options are all too positive.

9. **(3) sell Mr. Allen her part in the business** (Application) Selling her part of the business would include settlements for the distribution of profit and debt. Both partners are responsible until the partnership is dissolved; therefore, options (1) and (2) are false. Neither option (4) nor option (5) affects the legal partnership.

10. **(4) getting large loans from banks** (Application) A bank may have reservations about lending a large sum of money to an individual because only one person bears the responsibility of repayment. Options (1) and (2) are wrong because they are benefits and not problems. The problems in options (3) and (5) apply to any business, not just a sole proprietorship.

11. **(3) The ownership of the shares would be transferred to any heirs, who could either keep or sell them.** (Analysis) Because a corporation is a separate legal entity, it would not be affected as stated in options (1) and (5). Individual ownership of stock eliminates the possibility of options (2) and (4) because ownership extends to the stock alone.

12. **(1) The establishment and management of a corporation is more complex than that of a partnership.** (Evaluation) A corporation involves more legal work, and with a number of owners, a more complex management arrangement than the other types of business. No evidence is provided in the definitions for options (2), (3), (4), and (5).

13. **(4) Both Europe and Japan may have suffered an economic decline in the early 1990s.** (Analysis) Option (4) can be discerned from the graph, which shows a decline in motor vehicle production for Europe and Japan. The remaining options are either factually incorrect (1) and (2) or unsupported by the evidence (3) and (5).

14. **(3) Automobile dealers lower prices and offer cash rebates in order to increase sales.** (Application) This is the only option based on people buying more when prices are low and less when prices are high.

15. **(1) make the minimum wage lower for teenagers than for other workers** (Application) In effect, the "price" of teenagers (their wages) would decrease, so businesses (the consumers of labor) would want to hire more teenagers. The other options are not related to supply and demand.

16. **(1) They interact to bring prices to a balance point.** (Analysis) In the situation described, first the law of demand applies, as consumers buy houses when prices are low. But then the law of supply applies, as homeowners refuse to sell at the low prices. Fewer houses are available until prices go back up to a point at which owners are willing to sell. So the laws of supply and demand have interacted to bring prices to a balance point. Options (2) and (3) are wrong, since both laws operate in the example. Options (4) and (5) are incorrect, since in this example, the laws operate as they usually do.

17. **(5) find more outlets and make more cards** (Analysis) This would result in more profit. Options (1) and (4) would lower profits. Option (2) might be risky, and option (3) would not improve the business.

18. **(4) salt and pepper** (Application). The laws of supply and demand are not likely to apply much to products that are necessities, are used in limited quantities, and are cheap. A drop in the price of salt and pepper wouldn't lead people to buy more salt and pepper. In contrast, changes in the prices of options (1), (2), (3), and (5) might determine whether or not people would purchase those items.

19. **(1) taxes and fees levied** (Analysis) This option is the only one that is subject to local and variable control. The remaining options are either factors shared by different regions or are unsupported by the evidence.

20. **(1) an increase in products and services that use petroleum and its products** (Analysis) This option clearly relates to consumption and is broad enough to explain petroleum use. The remaining options are either contrary to common sense (3) and (4) or unsupported by the evidence.

21. **(2) Petroleum is used to produce fuels.** (Evaluation) This answer is implied in the passage. None of the other options can be derived from the evidence. Option (1) is contradicted by the experience of Japan. Options (3), (4), and (5) are unsupported by the information.

22. **(4) Japan** (Comprehension) The graph indicates that Japan saw a steep decline in prices from 1995-1997. None of the other countries saw an equally steep decline.

23. **(2) Out of sight, out of mind.** (Analysis) The author assumes that a product that is not made is not missed. Options (1) and (3) are the opposite of this assumption. There is no support for options (4) and (5) in the passage.

24. **(2) manufacturing** (Comprehension) The passage refers to the workers involved in the production of goods and distinguishes this group from all others, including agricultural and white-collar workers. The passage therefore assumes an economy is based on manufacturing, making options (1), (3), and (4) incorrect. Option (5) is wrong because it does not refer to domestic manufacturing.

25. **(5) demand for certain goods** (Analysis) The passage states that consumers would only marginally miss the goods that were not being produced. Options (1), (2), (3), and (4) are mentioned as definite results of low productivity.

26. **(1) depression** (Analysis) The passage mentions the depression as a major threat to businesses. Options (2) and (5) are wrong, because low production could lead to just the opposite—decreased spending and higher unemployment. Options (3) and (4) are not even mentioned in the passage.

27. **(2) The product itself is less important than the production of it.** (Evaluation) The author is not concerned with individual products but with the result of economic security. Option (1) is not supported with facts. Option (3) is wrong because it deals with values instead of economics. Option (4) is not suggested by the passage. Option (5) is wrong because the author sees capacity production as a foundation and not a cure-all.

28. **(4) income** (Comprehension) The highest correlation in the graphs is income. The remaining options are either factually incorrect or cannot be derived from the evidence.

29. **(4) High taxes are making it difficult for small businesses to succeed.** (Comprehension) The cartoon suggests that small businesses are being destroyed by high taxes. Option (1) is incorrect because the cartoon suggests small businesses are in danger. Option (2) is incorrect because the small business shown is not identified as a construction company. Option (3) is incorrect because the cartoon does not include any information about large businesses. There is no support for option (5).

30. **(5) a medical insurance plan** (Analysis) Only this option explains the payment mechanism, which does not allow for individual savings, but requires constant payment from workers in order to be eligible for future benefits. Options (1), (3), and (4) are individual plans that involve individual savings. Option (2) is not a plan, but a gamble.

31. **(5) Many long-term workers are losing their jobs.** (Comprehension) The number of people leaving the building on the right supports option (5). There is nothing in the cartoon to support options (1), (2), (3), or (4).

32. **(1) Large corporations no longer offer long-term job security.** (Evaluation) The signs in the cartoon indicate that large corporations are laying off people in long-term positions and hiring part-time workers to replace them. Options (2) and (4) are incorrect because the cartoon does not contain information about what kinds of jobs most people prefer. Option (3) is incorrect because we do not know that all of the people in the cartoon looking for part-time jobs will get them. Option (5) is incorrect because the cartoon does not contain any information about small corporations.

33. **(2) raise the CPI** (Comprehension) An increase in the price of oil would most definitely raise the CPI, because oil affects the lives of just about everyone. None of the other options is supported by the information given in the passage.

34. **(3) decreasing gasoline prices** (Analysis) Only this answer explains a drop in the CPI. If a major product decreases in price, the CPI will drop. Options (1), (2) and (5) cannot be inferred. Option (4) is irrelevant.

35. **(1) Increasing transportation costs might increase the CPI.** (Application) Only this answer would directly affect the CPI as described. Option (2) is unlikely, as is Option (5), since the improvements will cost the consumer and therefore affect the CPI. Options (3) and (4) are not supported by the evidence.

36. **(3) More Vietnamese products might be purchased by the U.S.** (Application) This answer offers an improvement for the Vietnamese balance of trade. The remaining options are either irrelevant or offer no clear improvement to the Vietnamese economy.

37. **(4) spending money no matter what their wages are** (Application) Option (4) is possible according to the figures on the graphs. Options (1) and (2) are not supported by the facts on the graphs. Option (3) is wrong because there is no information about specific dollar figures. The passage of time does not suggest option (5).

38. **(4) a change in the level of productivity** (Analysis) A drop in productivity would result in inflation and would affect earnings. Option (1) is unlikely, and option (2) would result in higher earnings. There is no evidence in the graph for option (3). Option (5) would not decrease wages but it would decrease net income.

39. **(1) have a lower standard of living than we do now** (Application) A continued drop in the value of money would result in less buying power. The correct option eliminates options (2), (3), and (4). Option (5) is too extreme.

40. **(1) Real earning has seen a net decrease.** (Evaluation) The hourly wage shown on the graph has decreased when it has been adjusted for inflation and expressed in 1982 dollars. The first graph shows a steady increase in spending which contradicts option (2). There is not enough information given by the graphs to support options (3), (4), and (5).

41. **(2) tools** (Application) Only tools are capital. Option (1) and (4) are labor. Options (3) and (5) are natural resources.

42. **(1) an oil company** (Application) Oil would be the primary expense. Options (2), (3), and (5) would have no expenses for natural resources. Option (4) is wrong because the major expense would be labor.

43. **(1) Some investment firms try to take advantage of senior citizens.** (Comprehension) The comment describes the investment firm's opinion of the potential customer and suggests how easy it would be to get her to invest. The other options are not clearly supported in the cartoon.

44. **(4) an advocate of consumer protection laws** (Application) The cartoonist objects to institutions taking advantage of people, senior citizens in particular, by playing on their fears for the future. There is no evidence for options (1), (2), or (3) in the cartoon. Because option (4) is correct, option (5) is eliminated.

45. **(4) stricter control of the money supply by the Federal Reserve** (Analysis) Economists who feel that business cycles result from flaws in economic systems would be more likely to support attempts to regulate things such as the money supply and inflation. All the other options propose ways of reducing outside interference in the economy, and so are examples of what someone who supports the second theory of business cycles would propose.

UNIT 5: Geography

Pages 45–55

1. **(4) Denver does not have an adequate water supply.** (Comprehension) If Denver had an adequate water supply, it would not need to divert water. Option (1) is incorrect because only the habitat is in danger, not the birds themselves. There is no evidence in the passage for options (2) or (3). Option (5) is wrong because the dispute is based on whether this statement is true.

2. **(3) a serious environmental problem** (Application) The abuse of water systems would seriously affect the environment. Option (1) incorrectly suggests expansion, not maintenance, of water-poor cities. Options (2), (4), and (5) have no support in the passage.

3. **(1) Human use of resources is more important than preservation of bird habitat.** (Analysis) The planners would be rightly concerned with people and believe the birds could land elsewhere, but option (2) would not convince the environmentalists. Option (3) suggests a wasteful use of water. Option (4) is false. Option (5) would involve persuading the cranes to go along with the decision.

4. **(2) strict emission controls in Europe** (Analysis) Only option (2) fits with the information, which blames auto emissions for acid rain. The remaining options are either irrelevant, (3), (4), and (5), or contrary to the logic of the question (1).

5. **(2) Southern and western states have seen a rise in aging population.** (Evaluation) The map supports this inference. It does not support option (3). The remaining options are either irrelevant or cannot be inferred from the information provided.

6. **(3) Alaska** (Comprehension) This answer follows from a comparison of states and use of the key. The remaining options are ruled out.

7. **(4) elder care centers** (Evaluation) Only this option is supported by evidence in the map. The remaining options may be true, but cannot be determined with the information given.

8. **(4) ranch style buildings** (Application) Hurricane winds would cause more damage to options (2), (3), and (5) than to low buildings. Option (1) is incorrect because the flooding would turn dirt floor cellars into swamps.

9. **(1) the air is warm and moist** (Analysis) Hurricanes are tropical and form over oceans, so they occur where the air is warm and moist. Options (2) and (5) are contradicted by these facts. There is no support in the passage for options (3) and (4).

10. **(2) shipping distances between the nations are quite small** (Analysis) Although Great Britain is separated from the continent by water (option 5), Western Europe is only about half the size of the United States, making international shipping fairly easy. There is no evidence for options (1) or (4) in the text. Although option (3) is true, it has nothing to do with the Common Market.

11. **(4) The natural boundary between Missouri and Kentucky is the Ohio River.** (Comprehension) The natural boundary between these states is the Mississippi River. The other options are true.

12. **(4) Cairo** (Application) Cairo is the only city that has direct access to both river systems.

13. **(4) 0° longitude** (Comprehension) Greenwich is at the Prime Meridian from which all longitude is measured; therefore, it would be 0° longitude. The Equator is 0° latitude.

14. **(3) ocean navigation** (Application) Latitude and longitude would provide points of reference on the vastness of the ocean. Option (1) would involve knowledge of the course of the river, not other coordinates. Each of the other options involves too limited an area.

15. **(3) Only lines of longitude are closer to one another at some points than at others.** (Comprehension) Longitudes come together at the poles and are farthest apart at the equator, while latitudes are at equal distances from one another. Options (1) and (2) are incorrect, because they are true of both latitudes and longitudes. Options (4) and (5) are wrong because they describe latitudes rather than longitudes.

16. **(3) Brunei** (Comprehension) Brunei lies outside the borders of Malaysia; it is another country. The other options are marked as cities on the map.

17. **(4) Indonesia** (Application) Indonesia shares a border with East Malaysia; this would offer easy access for trade. The other options would involve sea or air transportation.

18. **(2) Singapore was dominated by a Chinese, rather than a Malay, government.** (Evaluation) The government would be in constant conflict with the rest of the nation, so attaining independence would ease tensions. Option (1) is irrelevant. Options (3) and (5) have no geographic support. There is no evidence for option (4) on the map.

19. **(2) off-shore oil** (Analysis) The answer is suggested by proximity to oceans and extensive coastline. The remaining options are much less likely because of geographical location.

20. **(2) Florida's winters are somewhat cooler than its summers.** (Comprehension) Option (2) states a fact about temperature that is generally true over time. Options (1), (3), and (4) are incorrect because they are facts about a brief time. Option (5) states an effect of climate.

21. **(3) steppes** (Comprehension) According to the map, the steppe climate zones border both the north and the south sides of the largest African desert zone. Other options are not supported by the map.

22. **(4) desert** (Application) Desert areas lack water and are therefore rarely highly populated. This option is more likely than the remaining options, which suggest climates suited to habitation.

23. **(1) temperate** (Evaluation) The map shows that the northern-most tip of Africa is a Mediterranean climate zone. The passage indicates that the Mediterranean climate zone is temperate in nature. Other options are not supported by the map and the passage.

24. **(1) fish** (Application) Senegal's location with its coastline suggests fish as a possibility. Hydroelectric power (3) seems unlikely. Options (2), (4), and (5) do not reflect the climate conditions.

25. **(3) The proportion of young males, a group disproportionately involved in crime, has fallen.** (Application) The age of a population is part of what demographers look at. None of the other options is related to the basic characteristics of a population.

26. **(4) Disaster consultants in an area prone to earthquakes want to know if people living there are aware of precautions.** (Application) Option (4) relates to people's thoughts and actions. Options (1), (2), (3), and (5) all relate to age, distribution, and growth of a population.

27. **(4) Indiana has a land area of 35,932 square miles.** (Comprehension) Option (4) is the only option that is not concerned with the population.

28. **(4) Technology has affected the environment in many ways.** (Evaluation) Only in recent decades have scientists realized that significant changes in Earth's temperatures might result from burning fossil fuels. Option (2) is contradicted by the passage. Options (1), (3), and (5) are not supported by the passage.

29. **(2) find alternate sources of energy** (Analysis) A replacement for fossil fuel would eliminate the problem. Option (1) still suggests using a fossil fuel. Options (3) and (4) are incorrect because they treat the symptoms and not the source. Option (5) does not deal with the problem at all.

30. **(4) the prevalence of Spanish place names in California** (Analysis) The area that became California was claimed by Spain. There is no support for options (1) and (5) on the map. Option (2) is incorrect because France had not yet acquired the Louisiana Territory. Option (3) refers to a later development.

31. **(1) Norway** (Analysis) This country seems remote from any of the major fault lines. The remaining options refer to countries in proximity of fault lines and thus are ruled out.

32. **(3) oceans** (Comprehension) Most of the dots are located either in the ocean areas or on land near the oceans. There is no evidence for the other options on the map.

33. **(5) Acapulco, Mexico** (Application) Acapulco, Mexico, is located on the Pacific coastline where earthquakes are concentrated. All the other options are not near the earthquake patterns.

34. **(2) Large-scale forest fires are frequent.** (Analysis) The Bureau of Land Management is concerned with conservation and would realize that recycling might reduce some of the logging in areas already stricken by forest fires. Options (1), (3), and (4) are true but do not explain the Bureau of Land Management's interest in recycling paper. There is no evidence for option (5) in the passage.

35. **(3) Oregonians Don't Tan; They Rust** (Evaluation) The passage mentions the heavy rains in the west but does not refer to forest fires (option 1) or animals (option 2). There is no support for options (4) or (5) in the passage.

36. **(4) The Cascades block the wet ocean winds.** (Comprehension) The mountains tend to turn the ocean air currents back into the western valley. Option (1) would not affect humidity, and option (2) is a result of the dryness. There is no support for options (3) or (5) in the passage.

37. **(5) Idaho** (Application) Eastern Oregon borders on Idaho and would probably have similar crops. Options (3) and (4) are incorrect because they are midwestern states.

38. **(3) Africa and Latin America** (Comprehension) The graph supports this comparison. The remaining options are not supported by the graphic and thus are ruled out.

39. **(3) a slow decline in arable land per person** (Evaluation) Only this option can be derived from the graph, which provides information on the ratio between arable land and population, not on total arable land. The remaining options are either unsupported, irrelevant, or factually incorrect.

40. **(1) China** (Comprehension) Population in China rose over 190 million, an amount that dwarfs all other amounts. The remaining options are ruled out.

41. **(3) Thailand** (Comprehension) Thailand's largest city has 55% of its urban population in its largest city. The remaining options either have very low percentages of urban populations in their largest city, or a smaller percentage than Thailand.

42. **(4) Karachi, Pakistan** (Analysis) Pakistan's largest city has increased in this percentage over the last 15 years. The other options note a decrease in the percentage of urban population in the largest city. In addition, Pakistan's rate of growth is relatively high.

43. **(4) There is a lack of work in rural areas in many developing countries.** (Analysis) This answer can be inferred through common sense and by ruling out the other options. Options (1) and (3) contradict the assumption in the question. Options (2) and (5) are irrelevant.

44. **(1) The rates and patterns of urban growth are different in every country.** (Evaluation) Only this option is supported by the table. Options (2) and (5) may be true, but cannot be inferred from the table. Options (3) and (4) are generalizations that cannot be inferred or are not supported.

45. **(1) Thousands of people from different cultural groups arrived in America from 1871 to 1910.** (Analysis) An ethnic group is a national or cultural group. A variety of ethnic groups would result from immigration from the whole of Europe. Option (2) is too limited by cultural group and time frame. Option (3) refers to a result of the mass immigration. Option (4) is not an explanation of diversity. Evidence for option (5) is not available on the map, but the railroad construction would have been far from the cities.

46. **(2) the fact that over 3,015,000 people had immigrated from Southern Europe** (Analysis) Because Italy is a major country in southern Europe, it is reasonable to assume that a large percentage of the immigrants were Italian. Options (1) and (5) offer no basis for the statement. Option (3) refers to the wrong area, and option (4) refers to inaccurate information.

47. **(3) the Statue of Liberty** (Application) The Statue of Liberty is a symbol of hope and refuge. Options (1), (2), (4), and (5) represent specific historical events and persons rather than a general ideal.

48. **(2) Shortly after the turn of the century, language barriers forced many new arrivals into low-paying factory jobs.** (Evaluation) Most of the immigrants during this time did not speak English. Because the previous twenty years brought an influx of immigrants into American cities, there was little skilled employment available. The map does not support option (1). There is no evidence for options (3), (4), or (5) on the map.

49. **(5) how far you will have to travel** (Evaluation) A mileage or distance scale is missing from the map. All other options can be determined from the information provided.

50. **(4) Panama's length extends from east to west.** (Evaluation) The only way the Pacific end can be east of the Atlantic end is if the canal runs from the northwest in the Atlantic to the southeast in the Pacific. This is possible because Panama's length runs east to west, or parallel to the Equator. Options (1) and (2) are geographically false. Option (3) would make the statement impossible. There is no evidence in the text for option (5).

51. **(2) rapid population growth** (Analysis) Rapid population growth leads to a need for more food and firewood. Meeting these needs leads to a clearing of the land and eventually to desertification. The other options would not increase human use of the land.

52. **(1) Africa** (Comprehension) According to the map, Africa's desert area is visibly larger than that of other continents. Other options are incorrect.

SIMULATED TEST A

Pages 57–70

1. **(5) major patterns of vegetation** (Comprehension) The only information given is for the major patterns of vegetation. There is no reference on the map for any of the other options.

2. **(4) approximately 15° S, 60° W** (Analysis) The least attractive area according to the map is the pantanal which floods yearly. Options (2) and (3) are not only cities, but they appear to be in favorable locations. The Equator, option (1) runs through the rain forest and is probably more enjoyable than the pantanal. Option (5) is the location of S. J. Campos in the tropical forest. Both maps must be used to determine the location of the pantanal.

3. **(5) hot and wet** (Evaluation) The Equator is one of the warmest regions of Earth. The forest would most likely be hot and would, therefore, eliminate the other options.

4. **(2) the largest South American country** (Comprehension) The map clearly shows that Brazil is the largest country in South America. The other options are not true.

5. **(3) Brazil's natural resources have not been fully exploited.** (Evaluation) The large forests constitute a major resource; if they had been fully exploited, they would not figure so prominently on the map. Therefore, option (2) is wrong. The map does not provide sufficient information to determine options (1), (4), or (5).

6. **(3) The pantanal floods annually.** (Analysis) This option connects the landscape to the geographic needs of a hydroelectric plant. Options (1) and (4) speak of areas not located near the plant. Options (2) and (5) are irrelevant.

7. **(3) Individual efforts to combat environmental problems are threatened by even larger environmental ills.** (Evaluation) The small effort to have chemical-free food is in danger because the air itself is toxic. Option (1) is wrong because the garden itself is not the problem. Option (2) is not suggested. There is no evidence for options (4) and (5).

8. **(3) Buffalo were killed as white civilization moved westward.** (Application) None of the other options can be concluded from the photo.

9. **(4) Slavery was well established by the time of the American Revolution.** (Analysis) Slavery in America began when the Virginia-colony Africans were denied their freedom more than 150 years before the American Revolution. There is no support in the passage for options (1), (2), and (5). Option (3) may have been true, but there is no evidence in the passage.

10. **(2) Slaves had been regarded for too long as property rather than people.** (Analysis) Slaves had to be regarded as human beings in order to be thought of as equal. There is no evidence for option (1) in the passage. Option (5) is unlikely. Options (3) and (4) would have had no effect on popular opinion.

11. **(1) the German people ignoring the actions of Adolf Hitler** (Application) The basic attitude is that someone who is sufficiently different can be treated less than human. This viewpoint allows people to overlook various types of cruelty, even if they do not participate in the act itself. Options (2) and (4) are wrong because they are both more political and less basic human rights. Option (3) is wrong because it reflects an opposing attitude. Option (5) is wrong because it does not deal with basic human rights.

12. **(2) He was a slave owner.** (Comprehension) This option is indicated in the passage. None of the other options are supported by the passage.

13. **(1) new medicines and no decrease in the birthrate** (Analysis) This answer must be inferred by eliminating the other answers and by using historical knowledge. Options (2) and (4) are not historically true, as both would have occurred in previous eras. Option (3) makes no sense in the context. Option (5) may be true, but is not directly relevant to the issue of population.

14. **(2) economic drain of military campaigns** (Application) This answer requires applying the implied financial drain of the Crusades to general knowledge of the Medieval Church as an institution. Options (1) and (5) are not relevant to the Church's power in its own dominion. Options (3) and (4) are either unsupported or irrelevant.

15. **(4) The Crusades were a foolish military adventure.** (Analysis) This answer requires analyzing the language of the answers: foolish is a subjective word. The remaining options are facts.

16. **(3) Tripoli** (Analysis) The answer requires analysis of the map together with information from the passage. Tripoli is found between Antioch and Jerusalem. The remaining cities are either outside the regions of the Crusades or not deemed Crusader states.

17. **(2) The Crusaders were unable to "save" Jerusalem from the "infidels."** (Evaluation) Although Constantinople was sacked, the Crusaders were repelled quickly. The passage supplies this information. The remaining options are either irrelevant or historically incorrect.

18. **(1) Neither the Second nor Third Crusade succeeded.** (Analysis) From the fact that the passage and map focus on the First and Fourth Crusades, it can be assumed that there were Second and Third Crusades, making option (2) incorrect, and that both of them failed, making option (3) wrong. Options (4) and (5) cannot be inferred from the information given.

19. **(2) Small farms are disappearing.** (Analysis) This answer explains the twin trends in each graph. Options (1) and (3) are factually incorrect. Option (4) cannot be inferred from the graphs. Option (5) falls short of the analysis possible by comparing the two graphs.

20. **(4) Citizens of Nordic countries believe more fervently in equality of the sexes than citizens of other regions.** (Evaluation) This answer requires evaluating the data and the answers for an hypothesis rather than factual information. This hypothesis might find the number of women in Nordic parliaments as support. The remaining options are either facts or unsubstantiated inferences.

21. **(4) institution of child labor laws** (Application) The child depicted would no longer work under modern child labor laws. Options (1) and (2) are only indirectly related to children. Options (3) and (5) are not directly related to labor issues.

22. **(3) Some individuals profited at the expense of other people's labor.** (Comprehension) There is a clear difference between the well-dressed man and the workers. That he is in the lead suggests that he has control over them and uses them to make money. The facial expressions of the workers indicate that option (1) is wrong. Although options (2) and (4) may be true statements, they are not referred to in the cartoon. There is no evidence in the cartoon for option (5).

23. **(3) a check written on an approved bank form** (Application) A check written on a bank form is the only equivalent of cash listed. Options (1) and (2) are wrong because they are not backed by the government. Options (4) and (5) are simply records of financial transactions.

24. **(2) Our society has become too complex to trade on an item-per-item basis.** (Analysis) Too many items would have to be traded back and forth to get all the goods and services necessary for life today. Options (1), (4), and (5) may be true, but they are the results and not the cause of the abandonment of barter. There is no evidence for option (3) in the passage. People can be cheated in any system of exchange.

25. **(4) Europe** (Comprehension) The table shows that the combined reserves of European countries is greater than that of North American countries. The remaining options are not supported by the chart.

26. **(1) There would be a limit on the number of bills printed.** (Application) The answer requires understanding the effect of a "one-to-one correspondence." Options (2), (3), and (4) are unlikely. Option (5) is unsupported.

27. **(1) Argentina** (Analysis) According to the Charter, "A retiring member shall not be eligible for immediate re-election." Accordingly, all the options are eligible for re-election except Argentina, which has a term expiring in 2000.

28. **(4) The proposition will not pass.** (Analysis) In non-procedural matters, a permanent member may exercise a veto by not concurring, as stated in part 3 of Article 27. The remaining options are therefore either factually incorrect or unsupported.

29. **(2) It will pass if nine other members support it.** (Analysis) Unlike substantive matters, procedural matters cannot be vetoed by the permanent members. Options (3) and (4) are incorrect. Options (1) and (5) are unsupported.

30. **(3) They must abstain.** (Application) The parties must abstain if they are involved in the matter. A clear reading of the charter precludes options (1), (2) and (4). Option (5) is illogical.

31. **(1) The country must be a member state but not one of the Permanent Members.** (Comprehension) This answer fits the criteria laid out in the Charter. Options (2), (3) and (5) are illogical. Option (4) is prohibited by the Charter.

32. **(4) Belgium, Denmark, Germany** (Analysis) The desire for "equitable geographical distribution" suggests that countries from the same region might not serve at the same time. Options (1) and (5) are irrelevant, since they contain permanent members. The remaining options might well represent geographically distributed countries.

33. **(5) The percentage of voter participation dropped quite a bit when 18- to 20-year-olds were given the right to vote.** (Evaluation) None of the other options are supported by or can be inferred from the table.

34. **(3) Women have increased while men have decreased in participation.** (Comprehension) The graph shows an overall increase from beginning to end in participation by women and a clear decrease in the participation by men. The remaining options are factually incorrect or, in the case of Option (5), unsupported.

35. **(4) free elections** (Evaluation) Free elections would undermine a totalitarian government's authority. Option (1) is wrong because media would be controlled. There is insufficient evidence in the text for options (2), (3), and (5).

36. **(3) The early 1990s was a period of economic recession.** (Comprehension) The high unemployment rates of the early 1990s indicate a recession. Options (1), (2), and (4) are not supported by the graph. Option (5) is incorrect since unemployment rates were fairly low in 1999.

37. **(1) Many criminals are back on the streets because the prisons cannot hold all those convicted.** (Comprehension) The word overflow suggests that there is no room in the prison for all the prisoners assigned to it. Options (2) and (3) are wrong because there is no evidence in the cartoon of rehabilitation programs. There is no support in the cartoon for options (4) and (5).

38. **(3) international politics** (Evaluation) The students were not aware of a major political situation. Although the other options may be true, there is no evidence of them in this passage.

39. **(2) Lowering prices will increase demand.** (Analysis) The answer requires understanding the relationship between price and demand. The remaining options are not supported by the passage.

40. **(3) Tourism increased in the five years covered by the graph.** (Analysis) The graph shows this overall trend. The remaining options are either unsupported or factually incorrect.

41. **(1) It might serve to unify the country.** (Analysis) This answer is implied by the passage and by the needs of the business community. Options (2) and (4) are unlikely. Options (3) and (5) are irrelevant.

42. **(3) there was only a short portage between the Missouri and Columbia rivers** (Comprehension) As indicated on the map, there is a large amount of land between the Missouri and the Columbia rivers, which the explorers did not count on. None of the other options is supported by the information provided.

43. **(2) Spring and summer are the best time to travel.** (Analysis) The expedition stopped for the winter ("wintered") because then they could start anew in the spring. Options (1) and (5) are illogical. Option (3) is impossible, since the explorers had not yet met Sacagawea. Option (4) cannot be inferred.

44. **(2) It was located at the juncture of the Mississippi and Missouri rivers.** (Analysis) The proximity of St. Louis to these two major rivers made it the perfect starting-off point for the expedition. The remaining options are factually incorrect or cannot be supported.

45. **(5) a continuous water passage does not exist** (Application) The answer is implied by the use of the term *mythical* to describe the water passage. The remaining options are not supported by the passage and map.

46. **(3) They will try to work out their political differences.** (Analysis) In order for the United Nations to accomplish its goals, option (3) would be necessary. Options (1), (2), and (5) are unlikely considering the diversity of the members. There is no support for option (4).

47. **(1) Canada has a wide diversity of population densities.** (Evaluation). This answer requires understanding the information presented in the table. None of the other options is supported by the data.

48. **(2) Elected officials that PACs support in turn support the special interests.** (Analysis) PACs continue to operate only if their efforts are successful. Options (1), (4), and (5) have nothing to do with the increase of PACs. There is no evidence in the text for option (3).

49. **(2) Caracas was established by the eighteenth century.** (Evaluation) Only this option can be determined from the information given. Options (1), (3) and (4) cannot be determined. Option (5) is contradicted by the graph.

50. **(4) There is little chance of an economic recovery reaching the poor.** (Evaluation) Through his reaction to what many would consider good news, the man expresses the belief that economic recovery will not reach the poorest Americans. Options (1) and (5) are incorrect because the man would react more positively if he really believed in them. There is no support for option (2). Option (3) is incorrect since the man clearly places little value on the newspaper report.

SIMULATED TEST B

Pages 73–87

1. **(1) a bankrupt social security system** (Analysis) The hurricane bearing down on the house labeled "social security" suggests impending doom. Option (2) is too literal a reading. Option (3) is irrelevant. Options (4) and (5) suggest meanings that are contrary to the implication of the images in the cartoon.

2. **(1) that racism is part of American culture** (Analysis) The meaning of the cartoon might be, "Racism is as American as apple pie." None of the other options account for both the pie in the window and racism hiding in the basement.

3. **(2) It essentially acts as a boundary between the wet and dry sections of the United States.** (Analysis) The 100°W meridian runs through the major aquifer in the middle of the country. Because to the east of the 100°W meridian there is an abundance of ground water as opposed to the west where there are few aquifers, it can be called the dividing line. Options (1) and (3) are wrong because the meridian does run across the major aquifer. There is no evidence on the map for options (4) and (5).

4. **(1) They can affect relations between friendly nations.** (Analysis) Canada feels that its neighbor is acting irresponsibly. Option (2) is not suggested by the accusation. Option (3) is wrong because it suggests all pollution problems are caused by the United States. Options (4) and (5) have no support in the text.

5. **(2) Stalin's nonagression pact with Hitler left his country unprepared for the possibility of war with Germany.** (Analysis) This answer is supported by the explanation of Stalin's late reaction to the invasion. Options (1) and (5) are factually untrue. Options (3) and (4) are unsupported by the evidence.

6. **(3) the coming winter** (Analysis) This answer is implied by the reference to freezing conditions around Leningrad. Options (1) and (5) are unsupported by the evidence. Option (4) would not logically have helped the Soviets. Option (2) is unlikely, given the evidence that Stalin's leadership was belated and confused.

7. **(4) Iceland** (Comprehension) Of the options, the map indicates that only Iceland was allied. The remaining options were either occupied or neutral.

8. **(4) Soviet troops must have held at Stalingrad, because no German troops advanced beyond this point.** (Evaluation) The answer requires an examination of evidence from both the passage and the map. Options (1), (2), (3), and (5) are unsupported by the evidence. The map and the passage together help us determine the answer through inference.

9. **(4) It was part of the Axis forces and was not conquered by Germany.** (Comprehension) The map key determines this answer. The remaining options are either factually incorrect or irrelevant.

10. **(3) Repeal of the 18th Amendment had broad-based popular support.** (Application) This answer requires attention to the photograph's implications and an understanding of the Amendment itself. Option (1) and (5) are irrelevant. Options (2) and (4) are not supported by the evidence.

11. **(1) They could not repay loans.** (Comprehension) The businesses failed because they had no way to pay their debts. Options (2), (3), and (4) were contributing factors but were not the causes. Option (5) has no support in the passage.

12. **(1) Markets for German goods fell.** (Analysis) The answer can be found in the reference to markets being "cut off." Options (2), (4), and (5) are unlikely. Option (3) may be historically true, but the answer is not directly supported by the text and cannot be inferred.

13. **(2) the reliance on credit** (Analysis) Germany had not only lost the war but had also lost a good deal of money. Options (1), (4), and (5) are not true. Option (3) did not occur until after World War II.

14. **(3) Whoever controls the economy controls the nation.** (Evaluation) The Nazi government under Hitler gained control of labor, and afterwards the people had little room to resist. Options (1), (2), and (4) may have some validity, but they are not supported by the passage. There is no evidence in the passage for option (5).

15. **(2) worry about the apparent weakness of savings and loan institutions.** (Application) Threat of a banking failure means loss of deposits. Options (1) and (3) are not true. Options (4) and (5) would not be influenced by the failure of the Kreditanstalt.

16. **(3) Citizens voted through representatives.** (Analysis) The answer can be inferred from the description of Rome's evolving republic and from the definitions that follow. Options (1) and (4) may be true, but are irrelevant (insofar as all voters in democracies also may vote their interests). Options (2) and (5) are factually untrue, given the evolution of the Roman Republic.

17. **(2) Neapolis** (Application) This answer requires an application of information from the passage to that of the map. Late in the Republic, all Italians (that is, outlying Rome) were awarded citizenship. However, citizenship would not have been awarded to inhabitants of far-flung colonies like Gaul (France) or the cities in the other options.

18. **(2) Londinium** (Comprehension) The answer can be discerned from observation of the map. Although Britain came under the domination of Rome soon after, as of 44 B.C., the map indicates that Roman domination did not extend to London. All of the other options name cities that were under Roman domination.

19. **(3) oligarchy** (Analysis) The definition of oligarchy most closely matches the early "republic" of Rome, insofar as it was essentially a government of the aristocracy. The remaining options cannot match the description of government provided.

20. **(2) Population showed a steady rise.** (Evaluation) Of the options, only this one is possible. Although the numbers are estimated, they still constitute data. A trend is definitely discernible. The remaining options are either factually incorrect or cannot be inferred.

21. **(2) Richard Nixon** (Analysis) The answer is supported by the picture of Richard Nixon and the quote, which refers to the Watergate break-in. The remaining options are incorrect.

22. **(1) The French comprise a large minority of the Canadian population.** (Evaluation) The answer is supported by the table. The remaining options are either irrelevant or factually incorrect.

23. **(2) President Polk acquired the territories of Oregon, Texas, and California.** (Application) The annexation of the territories convinced Americans of their own greatness. Option (1) is not a positive factor. Options (3), (4), and (5) do not have anything to do with the nation becoming a world power.

24. **(5) The Vikings invade various European countries.** (Analysis) The timeline suggests pattern of Viking invasions. Options (1) and (4) pertain to singular events. Options (2) and (3) or are not supported by the timeline.

25. **(4) will increase somewhat** (Application) The answer is determined by following the pattern established in the chart. Options (2) and (5) are possible but highly unlikely. Options (1) and (3) run contrary to the trend indicated by the chart.

26. **(2) The Canadian tax burden is high.** (Comprehension) This answer is evident from the labeling and the position of the taxpayers. Options (1) and (5) are irrelevant. Options (3) and (4) are illogical or overgeneralized.

27. **(3) Title IX had been in place for a generation.** (Application) The answer requires applying information about dates to the passage. Options (4) and (5) are attractive, but unsupported by the passage or irrelevant, given the need to nurture sports. Option (1) is speculative, and Option (2) is factually untrue.

28. **(1) the increase in immigrants from Latin America** (Evaluation) This answer can be derived from the ratio of immigrants shown in the graphs. The remaining options are irrelevant—(2), (3), and (5)—or too general (4).

29. **(4) a lowering of tax rates on high-income households** (Analysis) This is the only option that can explain the rise in after-tax income of all the options (although of course other factors may be at work, as well). Options (1) and (2) do not affect income. Options (3) and (5) would not affect high-income households.

30. **(2) a substantial increase in literacy in the United States from 1860 to 1900** (Analysis) The increase in literacy would boost newspaper sales. Libraries (option 1) would not affect newspaper readers. Options (3) and (4) would not have had a great effect. Although option (5) is true, it would not have influenced the development of newspapers.

31. **(2) why an American dollar and a Canadian dollar are often worth different amounts** (Application) The two currencies would vary according to national agreement. The exchange rate has little to do with options (1), (3), and (4). Option (5) might have been somewhat relevant if the businesses wanted payment in dollars.

32. **(2) Consumption and emissions are higher among industrialized nations.** (Evaluation). This answer is supported by the passage principally. Other options are not supported by the evidence.

33. **(1) Eastern Europe** (Comprehension) This answer is evident from the emissions chart. The remaining options are of regions that have seen increases.

34. **(5) Asia** (Application) The answer requires estimating and comparing numbers from the chart. Options (1) and (4) are not included in the chart. The remaining options will not experience as sharp an increase as Asia.

35. **(4) There will be high levels of economic activity.** (Analysis) The answer is supported by the passage. Options (1), (2), and (3) are not supported by the evidence. Option (5) is irrelevant.

36. **(2) the Ninth District Circuit Court of Appeals** (Comprehension) California is in the ninth district. Options (1), (3), (4), and (5) are wrong.

37. **(4) The population density is much lower than in the area east of the Mississippi River.** (Analysis) A smaller population would require fewer hearings. There is no support on the map for options (1), (2), (3), and (5).

38. **(1) the Third** (Analysis) None of the other options are correct.

39. **(3) the Seventh District Circuit Court of Appeals** (Application) Both Chicago and Indiana are in the seventh district. Even if the two were in different districts, a case is appealed in the district in which it was tried. All the other options are wrong.

40. **(5) Property tax monies help support both county and city government**. (Comprehension) Substantial amounts of money go to both county and city governments. None of the other options are supported by the graphic.

41. **(1) Property taxes are based on the value of the home.** (Comprehension) The inclusion of the price of the home implies that property taxes are based on home value. Options (2) and (5) are opposite of what the caption implies. Options (3) and (4) are not supported by the caption.

42. **(5) It is impossible to tell, since we have no information about the ratio of students to tax dollars.** (Analysis) This answer requires analysis of the chart and an understanding of the question. The remaining options are based on a faulty premise.

43. **(4) Property tax revenues help support the schools.** (Analysis) The graphic shows that property tax revenues are spent on education. The remaining options are opinions.

44. **(1) to resolve major differences between the House and Senate over legislation** (Application) Disagreement between the House and Senate would be a matter that would have to be resolved. Although the other options might be handled by a joint committee, none is as important as option (1).

45. **(5) The map and the passage suggest that the Great Lakes facilitated transportation.** (Evaluation) This answer is particularly supported by the passage, which mentions the British Navy. The remaining options are either unsupported or, in the case of options (3) and (4), factually wrong.

46. **(1) The French were hampered by inadequate naval support.** (Evaluation) This conclusion can be inferred from the passage. The remaining options are either unsubstantiated opinions (2) and (5) or factually wrong.

47. **(1) The map does not provide information about the boundary.** (Evaluation) This answer acknowledges that there is insufficient information to make this conclusion. Indeed, the map shows only a portion of Canada and the U.S. The remaining options are either factually incorrect or unsupported.

48. **(3) It led to friction between the colonists and Britain.** (Analysis) This conclusion can be drawn from the final sentence of the passage. The remaining options are either factually incorrect —(1), (2), and (4)— or unsupported (5) by the information.

49. **(2) They are bad for consumers.** (Comprehension) The answer is clear from the labels and the position of the consumer. The remaining options are either overgeneralizations (1) or irrelevant (3), (4), and (5).

50. **(1) The consumer's budget is stretched to its limit.** (Evaluation) The consumer's budget is stretched tight very much like an inflated balloon. If any more pressure is applied, it will burst. Options (2) and (3) are incorrect. Options (4) and (5) are true but do not explain the appropriateness of the word inflation.

Answer Sheet

SOCIAL STUDIES

Name: _____ Class: _____ Date: _____

○ Simulated Test A   ○ Simulated Test B

1 ① ② ③ ④ ⑤	11 ① ② ③ ④ ⑤	21 ① ② ③ ④ ⑤	31 ① ② ③ ④ ⑤	41 ① ② ③ ④ ⑤
2 ① ② ③ ④ ⑤	12 ① ② ③ ④ ⑤	22 ① ② ③ ④ ⑤	32 ① ② ③ ④ ⑤	42 ① ② ③ ④ ⑤
3 ① ② ③ ④ ⑤	13 ① ② ③ ④ ⑤	23 ① ② ③ ④ ⑤	33 ① ② ③ ④ ⑤	43 ① ② ③ ④ ⑤
4 ① ② ③ ④ ⑤	14 ① ② ③ ④ ⑤	24 ① ② ③ ④ ⑤	34 ① ② ③ ④ ⑤	44 ① ② ③ ④ ⑤
5 ① ② ③ ④ ⑤	15 ① ② ③ ④ ⑤	25 ① ② ③ ④ ⑤	35 ① ② ③ ④ ⑤	45 ① ② ③ ④ ⑤
6 ① ② ③ ④ ⑤	16 ① ② ③ ④ ⑤	26 ① ② ③ ④ ⑤	36 ① ② ③ ④ ⑤	46 ① ② ③ ④ ⑤
7 ① ② ③ ④ ⑤	17 ① ② ③ ④ ⑤	27 ① ② ③ ④ ⑤	37 ① ② ③ ④ ⑤	47 ① ② ③ ④ ⑤
8 ① ② ③ ④ ⑤	18 ① ② ③ ④ ⑤	28 ① ② ③ ④ ⑤	38 ① ② ③ ④ ⑤	48 ① ② ③ ④ ⑤
9 ① ② ③ ④ ⑤	19 ① ② ③ ④ ⑤	29 ① ② ③ ④ ⑤	39 ① ② ③ ④ ⑤	49 ① ② ③ ④ ⑤
10 ① ② ③ ④ ⑤	20 ① ② ③ ④ ⑤	30 ① ② ③ ④ ⑤	40 ① ② ③ ④ ⑤	50 ① ② ③ ④ ⑤